Guide to Best Practices
for New School Administrators

Sheila E. Sapp

The Scarecrow Press, Inc.
Technomic Books
Lanham, Maryland, and London
2000

SCARECROW PRESS, INC.
Technomic Books

Published in the United States of America
by Scarecrow Press, Inc.
4720 Boston Way, Lanham, Maryland 20706
http://www.scarecrowpress.com

4 Pleydell Gardens, Folkestone
Kent CT20 2DN, England

British Library Cataloguing in Publication Information Available

Library of Congress Cataloging-in-Publication Data
Sapp, Sheila E.
    Guide to best practices for new school administrators / Sheila E. Sapp.
        p. cm.
    Includes bibliographical references.
    ISBN 0-8108-3743-9 (pbk. : alk. paper)
    1. School administrators—In-service training—United States—Handbooks, manuals, etc.
 2. School management and organization—United States—Handbooks, manuals, etc. 3.
Sapp, Sheila E. I. Title.

    LB1738.5 .S36   2000
    371.2'011'0973—dc21   99-056798

♾TM The paper used in this publication meets the minimum requirements of
American National Standard for Information—Sciences—Permanence of
Paper for Printed Library Materials, ANSI/NISO Z39.48–1992.
Manufactured in the United States of America.

This handbook is dedicated to the following special people in my life:

Eva E. Henry, my mother,
Emmanuel Murray, my father (deceased),
Nicholyn, my daughter,
Everette A. Sapp, my husband,
and
Edith L. Simpson, my friend and colleague.

Contents

Preface / vii

Acknowledgments / ix

1 Getting Started / 1

2 You Get What You Expect / 35

3 Getting Off on the Right Track / 49

4 Parent and Student Involvement Strategies and Techniques / 59

5 First-Year Lessons / 73

6 Survival Tools for First-Year School Administrators / 79

Appendix 1: Sample Forms / 83

Appendix 2: Sample "We Believe" Statements / 93

Suggested Readings / 99

About the Author / 101

Preface

Calls for educational reform, school improvement, and higher student achievement have spotlighted the role principals can play in meeting demands and educating the youth of today. School administrators and educational leadership students need a repertoire of skills, strategies, techniques, and resources to operate effective *and* efficient schools in American society.

This handbook was written to serve as a guide, resource, and handbook for new, veteran, and aspiring school administrators. Using my educational philosophy, basic beliefs about people, and firsthand experiences as a novice elementary school principal, I created and developed this handbook to help principals improve or strengthen their overall effectiveness as school leaders. Best practices, such as enhancing communication, developing short-and long-range goals, fostering a positive school climate, promoting professional growth of the faculty and staff, and increasing parent and student involvement help principals meet the challenge of running *effective* and *efficient* high-achieving schools. These best practices represent actual activities applied during my tenure as an administrator.

Principals, assistant principals, instructional supervisors, and college instructors can use this handbook as a source of strategies, ideas, techniques, activities, and practices to formulate plans to start the school year and implement the instructional program. Additionally, sample worksheets and activities are included that can be used as is or modified to meet various school, faculty, and staff needs.

New and veteran school administrators will have the opportunity to examine or reexamine their beliefs, values, principles, and philosophies of education as instructional leaders in their respective schools. College instructors may use the handbook to provide aspiring administration or educational leadership students with hands-on practical activities and experiences as they prepare for the principalship. Students may also use this handbook to gain a realistic perspective of the decisions, plans, procedures, and activities needed to manage and operate a school.

Chapter 5 describes a series of incidents that were very valuable, eye-opening, and in some instances, funny lessons. Chapter 6 contains some suggested tips for surviving your first principalship. The appendices include sample forms and belief statements, and the Suggested Readings section identifies resources for new, veteran, and aspiring school administrators.

Acknowledgments

It is not an easy task to mention all of the individuals, teachers, colleagues, professors, and friends who have helped me throughout my educational career. However, I wish to acknowledge Fenwick English, who suggested a publisher and shared several tips with me about writing a book.

I also want to use this opportunity to thank all of the auxiliary staff, teachers, parents, and students who unknowingly provided experiences and situations that helped me become a more effective and efficient school administrator. Finally, a special thank you to Noel Carroll, who saw something in me that I did not see during my first year as his assistant principal. His belief in me, support, and recommendation propelled me onto the road of school administration.

1
Getting Started

I remember that special day just as if it happened yesterday. The office manager summoned me to Dr. Carroll's office. As I stood outside his office door, a million thoughts ran through my mind. I wonder if a parent called? I did have to suspend a child from riding the school bus this afternoon. Soon Dr. Carroll opened his office door and ushered me inside. I sat down in the closest chair facing him, my mind still racing with thoughts as I leaned back in the chair.

"Sheila," he began. "The superintendent has asked me to open Mary Lee Clark Middle school in the fall. I will not be the principal here next school year."

My heart sank slowly to the bottom of my stomach as the meaning of the words became clear. I thought to myself, Oh no, this is my first year as an assistant principal, and I have really enjoyed working with Dr. Carroll. Now we will have a new principal to have to get to know. I was going to have to adjust to someone else! There would never be another person like Dr. Carroll! It was, however, his next statement that almost made me fall out of the chair in a state of shock!

"I am recommending to the superintendent that you take my place next school year."

"What!" I replied. "Are you serious?" Had I heard him correctly? I thought to myself incredulously. When I found my voice, I began to tell Dr. Carroll all the reasons why I could not take his place in the fall. For every excuse I voiced, he had a counter remark. He finally told me to think about it. I did, and after several days and nights of unrest, I decided to give it a try.

Before I realized it, I was faced with the task of beginning a new school year at the helm, not as the assistant principal. Weeks sped by as I contemplated the fast-approaching "first" day of preplanning and school. I was not quite sure where to start or how to begin. Finally, I purchased a writing tablet and spent the remaining weeks prior to preplanning jotting down thoughts and ideas. Reflecting on my life and educational career, I realized I had to make plans as one of the most important key figures in school—the principal. I suddenly realized that I had to really know who I was in order to lead others.

Who Am I?

We are the sum total of all of our experiences, beliefs, values, and principles. Our decisions and actions are governed by our inner selves, which will influence us for the rest of our lives. Sometimes we need to step back and take a good look at ourselves, take the time to rediscover who we are and why we have certain beliefs and values. Do you like who you are? If you don't like yourself, who will? We are made stronger by knowing our strengths and the areas in which we need improvement.

I developed "Mirror, Mirror on the Wall" (Worksheet #1) to help you take a closer look at yourself in a fun way. I strongly recommend completing the following activity on the worksheet provided or on a separate sheet of notebook paper before you read any further.

Worksheet #1

Mirror, Mirror on the Wall Activity

Directions: Stand in front of a mirror and look at yourself for ten to fifteen minutes. After viewing yourself, quickly jot down your thoughts in response to the questions listed below.

1. Who am I?

   _____

2. What five words would I use to describe myself?

   _____

3. What are my areas of strength as an individual?

   _____

4. Which areas do I need to refine or continue to develop?

   _____

5. What is my leadership style?

   _____

After completing your responses to the "Mirror, Mirror on the Wall" activity, reflect on what you have written for fifteen minutes. As you reflect, think about whether or not what you have written truly describes you as a person and professional. Try to be as specific and precise as possible. Remember, your inner self guides and influences your outer self, which is visible to the public, staff, parents, and students.

Philosophy of Education

Developing a philosophy of education is a very important activity for individuals involved with education. You will often be asked about your philosophy of education during your educational career. Sometimes you may wonder why it is necessary to have a philosophy concerning education. As an undergraduate student, all of my professors asked or encouraged me to examine my thoughts about education. Embedded in each of our philosophies of education lies our basic feelings and understandings about education. I found that my philosophy of education was largely based on the experiences I had as a student. Former teachers, colleagues, and my own personal experiences helped shape the educator I wanted to become.

Each of us probably remembers a teacher or teachers who set us on fire in the classroom. On the other hand, we probably also remember a teacher who demonstrated what not to do. It is hoped that we have had very few teachers that were poor role models. We can, however, learn meaningful lessons from both good and bad experiences.

On Worksheet #2, "My Philosophy of Education," which follows, write your philosophy of education, underlining key concepts and words. After you have underlined all of the key words and concepts analyze your philosophy of education by using the questions designed to guide your thinking listed on Worksheet #3, "Philosophy of Education Self-Analysis Questions."

Worksheet #2

My Philosophy of Education

_____

_____

_____

_____

_____

_____

_____

_____

_____

_____

_____

_____

Worksheet #3

Philosophy of Education Self-Analysis Questions

1. What do the key concepts and words mean to you?

   _____

   _____

2. Which key concepts will you emphasize?

   _____

   _____

3. What type of learning environment would your philosophy of education foster?

   _____

   _____

4. What impact will your philosophy of education have on curriculum?

   _____

   _____

5. Does your leadership style complement your philosophy of education?

   _____

   _____

Is there a match between your philosophy of education and the type of school you plan to lead? Frustration and stress will occur if no match exists between your leadership style and your philosophy of education. It is extremely difficult to support and be committed to basic principles or ideals that you do not believe. Your overall effectiveness as a school administrator is affected by your philosophy of education. All decisions and actions emanate from an individual's philosophy of education. Like the old adage says, "To thine own self be true." Never attempt to support or implement a procedure, school rule, or policy that does not complement your philosophy of education.

Principles and Values

Your principles and values are also critical to your development as an individual and as a school administrator. There will be times when your values and principles are tested. When you are in water up to your neck and surrounded by alligators, will you throw your values or principles out the window to travel the easier road or do what is more popular? What do you say to that parent, teacher, or colleague who asks you to bend the rule a little for a personal reason? They may say no one will ever know, because they will keep it in strict confidence! But, someone will know—you! You will have to live with the consequences of any decision you make. If you can easily set aside your principles and values, how will you be able to face extremely difficult ethical and moral issues?

Today we continually hear the cry for improved morals, values, and character. Individuals who have solid principles and values are sorely needed in education. Despite the technological and scientific advances we have made leading up to the twenty-first century, basic values and principles endure. It is our values and principles, in my estimation, that make us a caring and humanistic nation. Without values and principles, there is no hope for future societies and generations.

Following is a brief scenario of an incident in which my principles and values were tested.

I had a three-strikes-and-you're-out rule for handling misbehavior on the school bus. Parents and students were notified beforehand about our policy and the consequences of not following the bus rules. There was a third grader in our school who was notorious for getting into trouble. When the student committed his third offense, I held a conference with him and called his parents to inform them of their son's three-day suspension from the bus.

During my telephone conference, the student's mother pleaded with me to give their son another chance. I quickly informed the mother her son had been given several opportunities on different occasions to improve his behavior. I was simply following the school policy I had established. I could not treat her son any differently from the other children who had been suspended as a result of misbehaving on the bus.

The mother replied, "Well, I don't know how his father will respond when I tell him about the bus suspension. He'll probably be very angry and want to meet with you regarding your policy."

I responded, "That's fine, Mrs. Jones. Your son will still not be allowed to ride the bus. I will be happy to meet with your husband to discuss my decision. Would tomorrow afternoon at 3 o'clock be a convenient time? Please have your husband confirm the time with my secretary by tomorrow morning. Have a good day and thank you for your cooperation."

As I hung up the phone I wondered whether that had been a veiled threat or a warning? I was soon to find out that the father, like his son, also had a reputation. As a matter of fact, the father had been fired from his job after threatening to bring a bomb to work to settle a job-related dispute. I knew this was not going to be a pleasant parent conference, and I also knew I was not going to meet with the father alone in a closed office!

I could have taken the easy way out and bent the rules for this student so I would not have to face the wrath of this father. But would this have been fair to the other students who had been suspended? If I changed the rule out of fear, wouldn't I be acting contrary to a value I strongly supported—being fair? As the saying goes, if you don't stand for something, you will fall for anything!

I decided to handle this situation proactively. I contacted the school bus driver and director of transportation and requested their presence at the meeting. I also compiled copies of the school bus misbehavior referrals submitted to my office by the school bus driver. Parents also received copies of their child's school bus misbehavior referrals.

The wind was taken out of the father's sails when he was confronted with documented evidence and the school bus driver's testimony about his son's misbehavior. The conference did, however, end on a positive note, with the father making a commitment to help his son follow our system's school bus rules. After the meeting, Mrs. Hall complimented me on how well I handled the angry father and conducted the meeting.

"You were so calm," said Mrs. Hall. "I would have been very nervous dealing with that father because of his reputation. Weren't you scared?"

"Yes," I said. "I wore a long skirt so no one would see my knees knocking!"

Of course I was nervous, but my commitment to being fair gave me the added strength I needed to stand my ground. We cannot forget or forsake our values and principles for every situation or crisis that may arise. Stand firm, be true to yourself, and never let yourself down.

Your Beliefs

Have you ever taken the time to examine those thoughts, ideas, or feelings that guide your behavior and treatment of others? It is said that we are who we think we are. Many of our beliefs are the results of our environment, personal experiences, values, and principles. You cannot separate who you are as a person from your role as a school administrator. At the foundation of every action or behavior lies a basic belief. Beliefs give us the fortitude to support and stand up for what is right and best for teachers, students, parents, and ourselves.

One of my basic beliefs is that you should treat people the way you want to be treated regardless of how they treat you. Does this sound familiar? I also believe educators are servants of the public. As such, we must continually strive to serve and respond to our constituents daily. I know some days will be easier than others, but the important thing is to be consistent and fair in all your dealings with people. Over the course of several years as a school administrator, you will have a few classic "showdowns," but it is important that you always conduct yourself professionally and treat parents, teachers, and students with dignity and respect.

During my first year as a principal, I remember receiving a telephone call from an upset parent who alleged one of the custodians threw her son's brand-new glasses away. The mother insisted her son left his glasses on the corner of his desk before he went outside for recess. I told the mother we would check the classroom, playground, and trash can that afternoon.

The classroom teacher and her paraprofessional checked the classroom and looked in every desk after the students were dismissed. The custodians checked the playground and trash cans. Those glasses were nowhere to be found. I called the mother early the next day to tell her we didn't find her son's glasses. Being a wearer of glasses myself and also being guilty of occasionally misplacing my glasses, I asked the mother politely to check her house again for the glasses. I quickly explained that I wore glasses too and sometimes mistakenly thought I had put them in a certain spot only to find my glasses somewhere else. What did I say that for?

The mother immediately went into a long tirade. "I checked my house and those glasses are not here! Are you trying to say I don't keep a clean house?"

"No, I am not saying your house isn't clean. I do know that glasses can easily be misplaced in a house. It's happened to me numerous times as a child and as an adult."

The mother hotly retorted, "Well, if my son said he left his glasses on his desk, then that is where he left them! He does not lie to me. I paid $200 for those glasses and I want either the glasses or the money!"

As the loud click of the telephone resounded in my ear, I decided to write a check Monday morning if we still couldn't locate the glasses. The custodians, teacher, paraprofessional, and I spent Friday afternoon searching the classroom, playground, and trash for the missing glasses. Alas, no glasses appeared in spite of our efforts.

Early Monday morning, shortly after our opening exercises and announcements, I was greeted outside my office door by the paraprofessional who worked with teacher of the student whose glasses were missing. With a big smile that lit up her entire face, she handed me a note and said, "Mrs. Brown wants you to read this note from Jimmy's mother."

I read the note and burst into loud peals of laughter. I laughed so hard tears began to roll down my cheeks. Jimmy's mother had found her son's glasses in his older brother's book bag over the weekend. Mrs. Jones said that since Jimmy had not been truthful about where he had put his glasses, he was punished over the weekend.

Later that day Mrs. Jones called and apologized for her behavior and the things she had said during our telephone conference. That note and telephone call made my day! Although Mrs. Jones had been disrespectful and discourteous toward me earlier, I did not use this as an op-portunity to rub it in or make her eat crow. Instead I thanked her for letting us know she had found her son's glasses and for calling to apologize.

It was my belief about how one should treat people that kept me from responding to Mrs. Jones in the same manner in which she had spoken to me during our telephone conference. As a result of my conscious decision to do what was right regardless of how I was treated, I gained a priceless memory that I could bring to mind on the days I really needed something to laugh about. Be true to your beliefs and let them guide you for the rest of your life.

Use the next ten to fifteen minutes to write down your beliefs on Worksheet #4 or on a separate sheet of notebook paper. I challenge you to study and review your beliefs daily to evaluate your actions as a school administrator throughout the school year. Are you actually doing what you really believe?

Worksheet #4

My Beliefs

Directions: Write your beliefs about people, learning, school, teachers, students, parents and parent involvement, communication, and community.

People _____

_____

Learning _____

_____

School _____

_____

Teachers _____

_____

Students _____

_____

Parents _____

_____

Parent Involvement _____

_____

Communication _____

_____

Community _____

_____

Developing School-Wide Belief Statements

You've heard the saying, "Birds of a feather flock together." Well, I say, staff members with similar beliefs will flock together too. It is easier to accomplish school goals when there is a common bond unifying teachers, auxiliary staff, parents, and students. Generally, people are more supportive and committed to goals, projects, and school policies when they have a stake in the outcomes. Just as it is important for you to know your beliefs, it is equally important for your staff to know and be aware of the beliefs they have in common as a faculty. As educators, we have more things in common than we realize. How much time do you and your staff spend sharing beliefs about people, learning, students, parents, parent involvement, school, and community involvement?

By modifying the above activity, you can guide your staff through a process that will be not only enlightening but also fun. The best time to conduct this activity is prior to preplanning. Ideally you should gather your faculty and staff together a week or two weeks before school opens, when they are fresh and vibrant from their summer vacation and filled with excitement and anticipation. Of course, in order to do this, you will have to plan ahead and get agreement from your staff before school is dismissed the previous school year. Faculty and staff think best when they have the freedom to do so without the encumbrances of a regular school day or preplanning activities. So, if you can gain their support before the school year ends, half of the battle is over! If for some reason you are unable to meet the weeks before school begins, you can use staff development, preplanning, or postplanning days to develop school-level belief statements. The time you spend conducting and doing these activities will have far-reaching results. Your school will have a set of common beliefs that will guide decisions, behavior, and instructional activities for the entire school year. Think of how much could be accomplished if everyone is on the same wavelength and is striving toward common goals!

Directions for School-Wide Beliefs Activity— Phase One

Begin the activity by encouraging small group dialoguing among your staff. To accomplish this task, randomly divide your faculty and staff into groups of ten, ensuring that the groups are as diverse as possible. It is important that the group size is highly conducive to interaction and good eye contact. Instruct each group to select a recorder and a reporter. Copy and distribute Worksheet #5 for this warm-up exercise titled, "Getting to Know You."

Allow the groups five minutes to list things they have in common. (You can adjust the time to meet the needs of your staff.) To add some fun and interest to the exercise, offer a prize for the group that finds the most things in common within the specified time limit. After the group warm-up activity is completed, ask the groups to share their lists and briefly discuss the strategies they used for finding the things they have in common.

As the "common things" are shared informally, group members should place a check mark next to those items mentioned by other groups. By completing this exercise, your faculty will not only find out what they have in common as a group but also what the entire staff has in common. This warm-up activity is an effective technique for opening dialogue among faculty and staff.

A variation of the above worksheet activity that may be used to discover commonalties among your staff is called "Find Someone." In addition to identifying things in common among your school staff, the "Find Someone" activity (Worksheet #6) can be used as an icebreaker for new staff members during preplanning or staff in-service workshops.

Use the items listed on Worksheet #6 or develop your own items. Allow your staff ten to fifteen minutes to complete the worksheet activity. After they have written their own responses to each item, direct your staff to find the people in the room who have the same responses as theirs. Note: They may write the names of more than one individual on their sheet. The main object of the activity is to see how much they have in common with other members of the faculty and staff. Listen as the noise level rises! Your staff will have loads of fun doing this activity and might possibly find several new friends during the process!

Worksheet #5

Getting to Know You

Group #_____

Directions: List below ten or more things your group has in common. You have five minutes to complete this activity.

Things We Have in Common

1. _____
2. _____
3. _____
4. _____
5. _____
6. _____
7. _____
8. _____
9. _____
10. _____
   _____
   _____

Worksheet #6

"Find Someone"

Directions: Answer the questions listed below. Find someone who has the same responses. Write their name(s) on the lines provided.

1. What is the month and date of your birth? _____

2. What is your favorite season? _____

3. Which holiday is your favorite to celebrate? _____

4. What is your hobby or pastime activity? _____

5. What is your favorite color? _____

6. What state were you born in? _____

7. What is your favorite dessert? _____

8. What is your favorite sport? _____

9. How long does it take you to get to work? _____

10. What college or university did you attend? _____

After completing the warm-up activity (Worksheet #5 or #6), begin the second phase of the school beliefs exercise. Note: I strongly recommend not attempting to do the warm-up activity and formulating school belief statements at one sitting. Allow time for your faculty and staff to reflect on other possible applications of the warm-up activity. Can this activity be conducted with their students? If so, how would they use the information gained in their classrooms?

Prior to conducting phase two of developing school-wide belief statements, write your beliefs for each of the aforementioned areas (Worksheet #4) in a notebook or on a separate sheet of paper. Do not share your personal beliefs with your faculty and staff until after the entire school-wide beliefs process has been completed, otherwise you may unintentionally influence your staff. It is important for them to develop their own belief statements. Remember that you are also striving for commitment and ownership of the belief statements developed by your staff. Besides, it will be very interesting to see if any of the belief statements generated by your staff are similar to your own.

Developing School-Wide Beliefs Activity—Phase Two

Use the same groups randomly formed during the initial warm-up activity. Distribute a copy of Worksheets #7-A through H ("I Believe") to everyone. The groups may keep the same recorder and reporter or assign different individuals. Direct individuals to write their beliefs for each area listed on the sheets. Note: The faculty and staff complete the worksheet individually. When this activity is completed, ask that individual belief statements be shared within small groups. Members should note similarities (if any) that may occur within their group.

The final task of phase two is to select belief statements that are common within each group and arrive at a consensus. The "I Believe" statements become "We Believe" statements in a small group setting. Note: Parents and parent involvement may be treated as either one area or two separate areas.

Provide each group with a copy of Worksheets #8-A through H ("We Believe") and other appropriate materials (see list of materials/supplies needed below).

School-Wide Beliefs Activity Materials:

1. Chart paper (one tablet for each area)
2. Black markers (one per group)
3. "I Believe" worksheets (#7)
4. "We Believe" worksheets (#8)
5. Masking tape
6. Pencils or pens
7. Scratch paper

The school administrator and his/her administrative staff should circulate among the groups to provide assistance, monitor the process, and answer questions (if needed). Make sure the group understands that at this time, their belief statements are working drafts. The staff will approve a final draft of all of the school-wide belief statements at a later time.

The recorder of each group writes the "common" belief statements on chart paper with a black permanent marker. Post the completed charts on a wall or bulletin board as each group finishes. Each group's reporter presents their group's beliefs to the entire faculty and staff. During this process, members of your faculty and staff may ask questions or briefly discuss the belief statements as they are presented before the group.

Worksheet #7-A

"I Believe"

People Belief Statements

Group #_____

Directions: Write your belief(s) about people below.

_____

_____

_____

_____

_____

_____

_____

_____

_____

_____

_____

_____

_____

Worksheet #7-B

"I Believe"

Learning Belief Statements

Group #_____

Directions: Write your belief(s) about learning below.

_____

_____

_____

_____

_____

_____

_____

_____

_____

_____

_____

_____

_____

_____

_____

Worksheet #7-C

"I Believe"

Students Belief Statements

Group #_____

Directions: Write your belief(s) about students below.

_____

_____

_____

_____

_____

_____

_____

_____

_____

_____

_____

_____

_____

_____

_____

Worksheet #7-D

"I Believe"

Parents Belief Statements

Group #_____

Directions: Write your belief(s) about parents or guardians below.

_____

_____

_____

_____

_____

_____

_____

_____

_____

_____

_____

_____

_____

_____

Worksheet #7-E

"I Believe"

School Belief Statements

Group #_____

Directions: Write your belief(s) about school below.

_____

_____

_____

_____

_____

_____

_____

_____

_____

_____

_____

_____

_____

_____

Worksheet #7-F

"I Believe"

Communication Belief Statements

Group #_____

Directions: Write your belief(s) about communication below.

_____

_____

_____

_____

_____

_____

_____

_____

_____

_____

_____

_____

_____

_____

Worksheet #7-G

"I Believe"

Community Belief Statements

Group #_____

Directions: Write your belief(s) about community below.

_____

_____

_____

_____

_____

_____

_____

_____

_____

_____

_____

_____

_____

_____

Worksheet #7-H

"I Believe"

Parent Involvement Belief Statements

Group #_____

Directions: Write your belief(s) about parent involvement below.

_____

_____

_____

_____

_____

_____

_____

_____

_____

_____

_____

_____

Worksheet #8-A

"We Believe"

People Belief Statements

Group #_____

Directions: Write your group's belief(s) about people below.

_____

_____

_____

_____

_____

_____

_____

_____

_____

_____

_____

_____

_____

_____

Worksheet #8-B

"We Believe"

Learning Belief Statements

Group #_____

Directions: Write your group's belief(s) about learning below.

_____

_____

_____

_____

_____

_____

_____

_____

_____

_____

_____

_____

_____

_____

Worksheet #8-C

"We Believe"

Students Belief Statements

Group #_____

Directions: Write your group's belief(s) about students below.

_____

_____

_____

_____

_____

_____

_____

_____

_____

_____

_____

_____

_____

_____

Worksheet #8-D

"We Believe"

Parents Belief Statements

Group #_____

Directions: Write your group's belief(s) about parents below.

_____

_____

_____

_____

_____

_____

_____

_____

_____

_____

_____

_____

_____

_____

Worksheet #8–E

"We Believe"

School Belief Statements

Group #_____

Directions: Write your group's belief(s) about school below.

_____

_____

_____

_____

_____

_____

_____

_____

_____

_____

_____

_____

_____

Worksheet #8-F

"We Believe"

Communication Belief Statements

Group #_____

Directions: Write your group's belief(s) about communication below.

_____

_____

_____

_____

_____

_____

_____

_____

_____

_____

_____

_____

Worksheet #8-G

"We Believe"

Community Belief Statements

Group #_____

Directions: Write your group's belief(s) about community below.

_____

_____

_____

_____

_____

_____

_____

_____

_____

_____

_____

_____

_____

_____

Worksheet #8-H

"We Believe"

Parent Involvement Belief Statements

Group #_____

Directions: Write your group's belief(s) about parent involvement below.

_____

_____

_____

_____

_____

_____

_____

_____

_____

_____

_____

_____

_____

_____

Gaining Approval of the School-Wide Belief Statements—Phase Three

Working together as a school to approve a final copy of the belief statements is the most important step of the entire process. It is here you want to make sure adequate time is permitted for discussion and reflection among your faculty and staff. If adequate time is allowed, your final "We Believe" documents will be a true and accurate representation of your faculty and staff. So do not get discouraged or disheartened if it takes more time than you anticipated to complete the last phase of the school-wide beliefs process. The additional time spent here will be well worth your efforts and energy.

Keep in mind that the final "We Believe" statements represent the heart and soul of your staff. Can you think of a better way to foster and nurture commitment and "buy in" from stakeholders? What can be more powerful than having an entire staff totally committed and focused on the same objectives or goals? Would there be anything that you could not accomplish with everyone on the same wavelength? Remember, a house united will not fall.

Divide your faculty and staff into small groups and assign each group a specific belief area. Instruct each group to write "We Believe" statements for their assigned belief area. Each group selects an individual to present its "We Believe" statements to the staff.

After each group has presented its assigned areas of beliefs to the entire staff, compile the statements and distribute typed copies of each area developed to every member of your staff. Instruct your staff members to discuss and review each area of belief as a grade level or as an interdisciplinary team. Be sure to include special teachers and auxiliary staff (paraprofessionals, custodians, office clerks, etc.) in this process. Assign special area teachers and auxiliary staff to one of the grade-level groups or interdisciplinary teams. Your staff may need one to two weeks to complete their reviews and small group discussions.

During a faculty and staff meeting, arrive at a consensus or vote on the final versions of the "We Believe" statements. As soon as the school's "We Believe" statements have been finalized, frame and hang them in highly visible places around your building. I strongly recommend including copies of your school's "We Believe" statements in your faculty and parent/student handbook. Everyone should know what your school's belief statements are. Every activity, project, action, rule, and school-level policy must support each belief statement developed by your faculty and staff.

Set aside a specific time each year for your faculty and staff to review and evaluate what you are doing, to determine whether or not there is a need to modify or adjust school policies to address changes in your school's staff, student population, and community. Be willing to let your staff, students, parents, and community give you feedback on how well your school's actions, policies, curriculum, behavior, and procedures match or support your school's "We Believe" statements. Sometimes we are not always doing what we say we are doing in our schools. Allowing input and feedback from various sources will help your school become a better place for your clientele. Feedback is an excellent mechanism for bringing about needed changes and can serve as impetus for promoting professional and personal growth for you, your faculty, and staff.

Once your faculty and staff have gone through the process of developing and formulating belief statements, they will be ready to work on developing school-wide short- and long-range goals.

Developing School-Wide Short- and Long-Range Goals

You have recently become the principal of an elementary school. It is the fulfillment of one of your dreams. As the instructional leader in your school, do you know where you are going? Do you have a vision of where your school will be two years from now? What would you like to accomplish? What will you focus your school's efforts on? How will you ensure increased achievement for all students in your school? In what direction would you like to see your school headed? Are there any curriculum changes needed? What strategies or resources will you use? These are just a few of possibly many questions that may come across your mind as you go about getting ready for the new school year.

Do you remember Dorothy in *The Wizard of Oz*? When Dorothy awakened in a strange land, she focused all of her energy and efforts on trying to find a way to get back home. Returning home to Kansas was Dorothy's short-range goal. Once she found out who could help her return home, Dorothy courageously followed the "yellow brick road," which led her to the Emerald City. As a result of her own efforts, along with the help of her friends (Tin Man, Lion, and Scarecrow), Dorothy was able to finally return home to Kansas.

Without a plan or road map to serve as a guide, new school administrators may wander aimlessly throughout the school year like visitors in a foreign land. Taking the time to think about where you want to go or what you want to accomplish will keep you focused and well grounded. Before you try to chart a course for your faculty and staff to follow, you need to know, as the building administrator, where you want to go and what you want to do. Do you have any personal or professional short- and long-range goals? When was the last time you sat down to write goals for yourself? If you have written short- and long-range goals in the past, are they still applicable now? Perhaps now is a good time to revisit and reevaluate your short- and long-range goals if you have not already done so.

To help you formulate your own short- and long-range goals, ask yourself the following two questions, which are applicable to personal and professional goals: (1) Where do I want to see myself one year from now? (2) Where do I want to see myself five years from now? Use Worksheet #9, "Personal and Professional Short- and Long-Range Goals," provided in this handbook, or a separate sheet of notebook paper to do the exercise.

Worksheet #9

Personal and Professional Short- and Long-Range Goals

Personal Short- and Long-Range Goals

1. Where do I want see myself personally one year from now?

   _____

   _____

2. Where do I want to see myself five years from now?

   _____

   _____

Professional Short- and Long-Range Goals

3. Where do I want to see myself professionally one year from now?

   _____

   _____

4. Where do I want to see myself professionally five years from now?

   _____

   _____

Once you have completed writing your personal and professional goals, you are now ready to guide your faculty and staff through a similar activity. During a general faculty or grade-level team meeting, instruct your staff to spend fifteen to twenty minutes in small groups discussing and responding to the questions on Worksheet #10, School Short- and Long-Range Goals. Follow the same procedures outlined in phases two and three to develop and formulate school-wide belief statements.

Try to get your staff to focus on two or three important goals. Selecting too many goals will frustrate you as well as the faculty and staff. Nothing builds confidence like success! Make sure several of your short-range goals are obtainable. Be realistic about the time, energy, and resources needed to help you accomplish whatever goals (short- or long-range) your staff targets for the school year. Actually accomplishing specified school-wide goals will motivate you and your staff to select and obtain additional short- and long-range goals.

Seek and obtain a balance between the number of short- and long-range goals selected each school year. Analyze each desired goal and determine what resources, manpower, materials, and technical assistance is needed or required to complete identified school-wide goals. Also, examine factors that may impede the attainment of your school's desired goals.

Rank your goals in priority order. Are there any goals that need to be completed before others? Is there a goal that will have an impact on another short- or long-range goal? Are there any goals outside your or your staff's span of control? Do you have direct influence on a goal or must you rely totally on the performance of others to obtain any of the desired goals?

Goals over which you have direct influence and that are within your span of control should be labeled short-range goals. Designate goals requiring more time to complete as long-range goals. Post a listing of the goals in your office as a constant reminder and point of focus. Use your goals to guide and direct all instructional and curricular activities in your building. Meet with your faculty and staff periodically throughout the school year to give them an updated status on the identified school-wide goals. Additionally, share the information with the parents at Parent Teacher Association meetings and community civic organizations. Always be prepared to spotlight your school at a moment's notice. Broaden your school's base of support by publicizing school activities and accomplishments. Generally, people tend to support what they know about and understand. There are many positive activities and programs going on in public schools that are not known or go unnoticed by the general population. Don't be afraid to toot your own horn and celebrate your successes!

Finally, involving faculty, staff, and parents in developing, formulating, and obtaining short- and long-range goals will foster ownership and commitment. A unified faculty and staff will be able to accomplish any goals put before them.

Worksheet #10

School Short- and Long-Range Goals

Group #_____

Short-Range Goals

1. Where do we want see our school one year from now?

_____

_____

_____

_____

_____

Long-Range Goals

2. Where do we want to see our school five years from now?

_____

_____

_____

_____

_____

2

You Get What You Expect

Your first year as a school administrator is probably the most exciting and rewarding experience in your professional career. I still remember how feverishly I planned that summer prior to my official first day as principal. I spent early summer mornings filling a writing tablet with ideas, strategies, and programs I wanted to implement during the school year. One afternoon while reviewing the notes I had written in my tablet, a thought suddenly hit me. I was planning all of these "things" for my school and had made very few plans for the most important part of an effective school—faculty and staff. There was no way I would be able to implement my tabletful of ideas if I did not have a willing and supportive staff. My plans would need to include faculty and staff as well as our students and parents.

All of my educational leadership instructors emphasized, on many occasions, how important it was for school administrators to get off to a good start. If you do not have a plan, then you are planning to fail. Does this sound familiar? Your first day as the instructional leader in the building will set the tone for rest of the school year. When you stand before your faculty and staff for the first time, all eyes will be focused on you. They will be trying to read and size you up, just as you will be reading and sizing them up. It's my belief that faculty and staff members should not have to resort to gazing into a crystal ball, reading tarot cards, or calling the Psychic Hotline to know or understand what you expect of them as their building-level supervisor.

Generally, you get what you expect. So, doesn't it seem logical to communicate your expectations in order to get what you want from your staff? If faculty and staff members know what you want, they will always know what is expected and where you stand. This is one way to eliminate or limit unnecessary frustrations and lackluster performance among your staff.

Let's not forget the other side of the coin, which is equally as important as communicating your expectations. Faculty and staff need to know what they can expect from you as the school administrator and their immediate supervisor. Sometimes we fail to tell our teachers and auxiliary staff what behavior and performance to expect from us. They need to know something about the administrator who will be leading them and the school. If everyone knows what to expect from each other, it will be easier to accomplish school-wide goals and objectives.

To develop expectations for your faculty and staff, divide them into the following areas: administrative (assistant principal, secretary, office clerk, etc.), teachers, and auxiliary (paraprofessionals, custodians, lunchroom personnel) staff. Expectations may also be formulated and written for students, parents, and other key groups or organizations, such as PTAs (Parent and Teacher Association) and PTOs (Parent and Teacher Organizations). Make sure you include any group of individuals who will be involved either directly or indirectly with your staff, students, and parents during the school year.

Start the process by writing the expectations or behaviors you expect from each of the groups in the aforementioned categories. Feel free to include additional categories if needed. When you formulate your list of expectations, try to limit them to no more than ten items. Select those expectations you feel are most important and key to fostering a school climate that supports your basic beliefs, values, and principles as a school administrator.

You may use Worksheet #11, "My Expectations," provided in this handbook, or a sheet of notebook paper on which to write your expectations. Following is an abbreviated "sample" list of expectations I used with my faculty and staff at Crooked River Elementary School.

1. Be on time.
2. Greet each student everyday with a smile at the classroom door.
3. Conduct yourself in a professional manner at all times.
4. Be responsive to students', parents', and citizens' questions, concerns, or issues.
5. Treat others the way you want to be treated.
6. Be proactive and *not* reactive.
7. Handle the little things, and let the administrators handle the big things.
8. Be kind and courteous to your colleagues and peers.
9. Say what you mean and mean what you say.
10. Keep school matters and issues in school.

Worksheet #11

My Expectations

School Year_____

Expectations for Administrative Staff

1. _____
2. _____
3. _____

Roles/Responsibilities of the Administrative Staff

1. _____
2. _____
3. _____

Expectations for Office Staff

1. _____
2. _____
3. _____

Roles/Responsibilities of the Office Staff

1. _____
2. _____
3. _____

Worksheet #11 (*continued*)

My Expectations

School Year_____

Expectations for Faculty

1. _____
2. _____
3. _____

Roles/Responsibilities of Faculty

1. _____
2. _____
3. _____

Expectations for the Auxiliary Staff

1. _____
2. _____
3. _____

Roles/Responsibilities of Auxiliary Staff

1. _____
2. _____
3. _____

Worksheet #11 (*continued*)

My Expectations

School Year_____

Expectations for Students

1. _____
2. _____
3. _____

Roles/Responsibilities of Students

1. _____
2. _____
3. _____

Expectations for Parents

1. _____
2. _____
3. _____

Roles/Responsibilities of Parents

1. _____
2. _____
3. _____

Worksheet #11 (*continued*)

My Expectations

School Year_____

Expectations for Parent and Teacher Associations/Organizations

1. _____
2. _____
3. _____

Roles/Responsibilities of Parent and Teacher Associations/Organizations

1. _____
2. _____
3. _____

Expectations for _____

1. _____
2. _____
3. _____

Roles/Responsibilities of _____

1. _____
2. _____
3. _____

Next, list things your staff can expect from you as the school administrator and instructional leader. Note: You and your administrative staff need to develop the administrative expectations as a team. While working as a team, create expectations mutually. Administrative team members must be supportive of each other at all times. Also, take time to share, review, and discuss your expectations with a mentor or trusted personal friend. Two or three heads are always better than one. Do not expect or ask a staff member to do anything you would not do. You must model the expectations or behaviors you want from your staff everyday throughout the school year. What you do speaks louder than what you say! Serving as a positive example is the best way to communicate your expectations to faculty, staff, students, and parents.

Another aspect of communicating expectations is outlining specifically and clearly what each person is to do—that is, their responsibilities. Although school administrators are charged with the responsibility of supervising and overseeing the total instructional program, it is a task that cannot be accomplished alone. Running a quality school requires the cooperation, support, and commitment of other individuals as well. School administrators should delegate specific responsibilities to school personnel based on the role they are expected to play as an integral part of the total school operation.

Ask yourself the following questions to help you generate and outline specific responsibilities for key individuals in your school.

1. What programs or areas do I need to delegate to ensure and protect my role as instructional leader in the building?
2. Which programs or areas do I need to supervise myself?
3. Are there any routine tasks that can be handled by the clerical staff?
4. Do the individuals have the knowledge and skills needed to perform their assigned responsibilities?
5. Are resources/in-services needed to help selected individuals perform their responsibilities more efficiently?
6. Have I realistically and fairly distributed the responsibilities among faculty and staff members?

After completing your list of specific responsibilities for specified individuals, share them with a peer or colleague for feedback. I found this to be very helpful. Sometimes you inadvertently omit important tasks that need to be assigned. Once you have reviewed your list, meet with the individuals and go over their responsibilities with them. This will be an opportunity to answer questions about the tasks assigned or request additional training (if needed). Give each individual a copy of their job responsibilities and keep a signed copy on file in your office. Be willing and flexible enough to make changes if there is a need to add or delete task responsibilities. I guarantee 95 percent of the time staff members will perform assigned tasks and responsibilities to your satisfaction. Individuals who are not performing as expected should be told so. Do not wait until a situation gets intolerable before you have a conference with the individual. People will never know they are not meeting your expectations if you do not tell them. Provide as much assistance and as many resources as possible to help an individual improve. If after a specified period of time there is no change in the individual's job performance, consider termination. If we are fair with people and try to help, there can be no hard feelings or negative claims when we are faced with terminating an employee (certified or noncertified). We must always do what is best for the students and the school. The faculty, staff, students, and parents are counting on school administrators to look out for the welfare of all clientele.

Lines of Communication

During those many weeks of planning for my first day as the principal, I never thought about communication or even developing a plan for communication in my school. After the first three weeks of school I realized I needed a communication plan. I was amazed at the number of telephone calls, requests for conferences, and appointments I received from sales representatives who just happened to be in the neighborhood and wanted to "drop in." Sometimes, when I returned to my office after early morning duty, I had ten or fifteen telephone messages or notes from staff members in my mailbox.

I spent several late evenings trying to respond to all of the telephone calls and requests for conferences that were in my mailbox. After several days of repeatedly trying to stay on top of all of my calls and conferences, I realized I was headed for Burnout City if I did not come up with a workable solution.

To get a better handle on things, I developed and implemented a procedure called "Lines of Communication" to channel the flow of communication in my school from staff, parents, and other concerned individuals. Specific times during the school day were set aside for meeting with staff and parent conferences. Every week I met with sales representatives from 8:00 a.m. to 8:30 a.m. Tuesday through Thursday. The office staff was instructed to schedule any salesperson who "dropped in" to meet with me during the specified time. If they really wanted to try to sell their product, they would make an appointment to see me. If not, they would simply leave the information with the secretary. Isn't that better than having your workday interrupted unnecessarily? I also set aside a specific time during the day to return telephone calls. Always return calls, unless it is humanly impossible, the same day. It is especially important to return the calls of a disgruntled parent or other individual right away. The longer they wait for you to return their call, the more disgruntled and angrier they become. Besides, it's just common courtesy to return calls. If you are unable to return the call personally, ask your secretary to call the individual and tell them you are in a meeting or another conference and that you will call them as soon as your meeting or conference is over. At least that lets the individual know you did receive the telephone message and you intend to return their call.

Have you thought about how you want communication to flow in your school? Do you want your staff, parents, and students to follow specific steps or procedures within the communication network in your school? These are questions that need to be considered seriously by new school administrators. Without specific lines of communication, it's difficult to keep up with requests for conferences, appointments, and responses to questions or concerns from parents. As far as I am con-

cerned, we must make every effort to respond to the public in a timely and professional manner. We are servants of the public and should continuously strive to serve their needs and respond to their questions.

Ninety percent of the requests for conferences and telephone calls I received dealt with parental questions and concerns regarding school policies, curriculum, and teachers. "Johnny has too much homework." "Why does the kindergarten team use 'time out' with their students?" "Mrs. Jones grades too hard!" "I think requiring children to do book reports in fourth grade is not appropriate." "My son feels his teacher does not like him." Do any of these questions or concerns sound familiar?

To help me get a handle on the questions, concerns, and requests for conferences in my school, I set up a specific channel of communication. I called these channels "Levels of Communication." The first level of communication begins with the classroom teacher. During those first few weeks of school, I found that the majority of the questions and concerns had to do with what Johnny or Susie was doing in the classroom. Many times parents do not discuss their questions or concerns with a classroom teacher before contacting the school administrator. I have held many conferences in which a simple matter could have been resolved if the parent had expressed his or her concern to their child's teacher. Many teachers want parents to give them the opportunity to answer questions or address concerns before they are presented to the school administrator. If I could collect a dollar for every time a teacher said, "They never discussed this concern with me," I would probably be a millionaire by now. The first level of communication was direct contact with the classroom teacher. Parents were strongly encouraged to schedule a conference with their child's/children's teacher before they called or consulted anyone else. Administrative and office personnel were instructed to ask parents whether or not they had conferred with the classroom teacher as the first screen when responding to questions or concerns. As you can see, it is much better to have the teacher address the concern initially since they actually work with the children in the classroom. Teachers develop specific strategies with the parents to address parental concerns. A parent conference form is completed to document the outcome of the meeting, and both the parent and the teacher keep a copy for their personal file. Also, a copy of all parent conference forms are filed in the Administrative Office. By keeping a file in the office, the administrative staff has a record of the number of parent contacts that have occurred. If by any chance, a situation or concern isn't resolved and ends up in the assistant principal's or principal's office, you will be able to read and review the parent conference form to find out what has already taken place.

The second level of communication is used when parents have consulted the teacher and continue to feel dissatisfied. At the second level the parent schedules a conference with the teacher, assistant principal, or guidance counselor present. Together the team tries again to resolve the issues or concerns. The classroom teacher and parent must agree on a mutually developed plan of action. Involving the parent during the action plan process gives them ownership of and commitment to the plan itself. The teacher and parent work as a team supporting each other in the classroom and at home.

The third level of communication involves the principal. This level is reached when levels one and two have still not resolved the issue, concern, or question. When conferences reach the third level, the school administrator can be certain that there have been other attempts and nothing has worked to the satisfaction of both the parent and the classroom teacher. The school administrator reviews the previous conferences and determines what the next step or strategy should be. All parties involved know that level three is the final attempt to resolve the concern. Additionally, all parties are bound to the final decisions made by the principal. Parents who are still dissatisfied are encouraged to schedule a conference with the appropriate central office personnel.

During my tenure as an elementary principal, the number of conferences that reached level three throughout the school year were few. Parents were pleased with our efforts to resolve situations and answer questions. We made every

effort to try as many different strategies as possible to keep a positive flow between the parent, school, and the child's classroom teacher. No stones were left unturned!

As a cautionary note I would like to add that there might be occasions when a situation may warrant skipping a level. You will have to use your own professional judgment and treat those situations case by case. If a parent, staff member, or concerned citizen shows up in your office madder than a wet hen and ready to explode, asking them if they followed the levels of communication steps may not be a good idea. I have found the best way to put a lid on those types of encounters is to see the individuals immediately in order to defuse the situation. So, depending on the circumstances and the client's state of mind, it is possible to begin at level three and later refer the client to level one.

Let me share one experience with you to illustrate my point. One fine Monday morning shortly after the opening exercises, I was in my office working on a report that was due to the central office the next day. I had closed my office door so I would be able to work without interruption. Just as I was beginning to work on the last page of the report, a knock on my door interrupted my concentration. I looked up as my office manager stuck her head through the door, apologized, and closed the door quietly behind her. As she made her way to my desk, I could tell by the expression on her face that she was a little disturbed. For her to interrupt me signaled a red-flag situation.

The office manager quickly gave me a brief description of the situation and stated that the parent out in the waiting area could not be reasoned with and she demanded to see the principal immediately. At that point my report lost its priority and was moved to the back burner. I got up from my desk, walked out to meet the parent, and escorted her into my office.

As I ushered Mrs. Brown to a seat at the round table in my office, tears began to trickle down her cheeks. I handed her a box of tissues as she began to apologize effusively for her loss of composure.

"I am sorry, Mrs. Hutchinson, but I am so angry with Tommy's teacher that if she was here right now, I would strangle her!"

Now you know I wasn't going to direct her at this point to meet with her son's teacher! My role immediately shifted into that of a listener and peacemaker. After Mrs. Brown was able to tell me calmly about what had upset her, I was able to get to the root of the problem. Mrs. Brown felt she was still too angry to discuss her concern with the classroom teacher, so I agreed to meet with the teacher. I then thanked Mrs. Brown for being honest and sincere about her feelings.

As I escorted Mrs. Brown out of my office and walked her to the front door of the building, we were laughing about a funny personal incident that I had shared with her. The conference lasted about an hour, but the time spent was well worth it! Not only had I found the key to resolving the situation, but I had also found something we had in common, a teenage daughter. I used what we had in common to help Mrs. Brown leave on a positive note. Also, because of the unusual circumstances, the situation was resolved without Mrs. Brown meeting with the teacher first. However, she was able to meet with her son's teacher after the teacher-parent relationship had been restored.

On a lighter note, I remember another situation that began at level three, which, in retrospect, was one of the strangest parent conferences I had ever conducted. One October day in the mid-afternoon, my secretary ushered a visibly agitated mother into my office. Immediately after sitting down, the mother began the conference with "I am not quite sure I know how to say this, but I think my son's teacher is a witch." I had to really restrain myself from making an exclamation of disbelief. I swallowed my immediate response and said, "Mrs. Brooks, why do you think your son's teacher is a witch?" I must add here that from time to time as a school administrator you do have to deal with individuals who have the reputation of being "extreme," but this person before me had had no such history. As a matter of fact, this parent was a lieutenant in the U.S. Navy!

"Well, his behavior has really been different for the past two weeks. He's gotten into fights in the neighborhood. He acts like he is possessed! Every time I meet with his teacher she is wearing black. Last night he had to write a scary story for a homework assignment. I am really concerned, and I really do not want to talk with his teacher about this latest development."

"Mrs. Brooks, Halloween is about two weeks away and I believe many of our teachers have had students write scary stories to go along with Halloween. Do you object to your son participating in projects related to Halloween in his classroom?"

"Oh, no! He enjoys the writing assignments. There's been such a change in his behavior lately that I have no idea what is going on. Would you please look into the matter?"

Mrs. Brooks was a little less nervous at the close of our conference. I told her I would contact her after I had had a chance to discuss the matter with the classroom teacher. I was bewildered as I sat in my office mentally reviewing my conversation with Mrs. Brooks. It was not everyday you had to tell a teacher that one of her parents believed she was practicing witchcraft and had cast a spell on her child.

Somehow I got through the conference with the classroom teacher. Mrs. Brooks' son had been experiencing difficulty with some of his peers in the classroom but not enough to warrant a referral to the office. The classroom teacher decided to discontinue the Halloween story-writing activity. She jokingly assured me she was not a witch. A behavior contract between the child and teacher curved the inappropriate behavior in the classroom. Mrs. Brooks did not come in again with any additional allegations. In this instance too, a level-three intervention was the best way to deal with the situation. Can you imagine the response of the teacher if she had been hit with the "witch" accusation firsthand? Oh, by the way, the teacher did like wearing black.

Level three interventions can pave the way for successful level one lines of communication. The Levels of Communication are excellent guides, but you should always be willing to skip a level if the circumstances or situations warrant it. It is extremely important that some system of communication be established, whether or not you decide to use the procedure I developed for my school. A school not equipped to handle or address questions or concerns cannot be receptive to community members, staff, parents, or students. The three levels of communication I developed are as follows:

Level One—classroom teacher
Level Two—classroom teacher, parent, assistant principal, or counselor
Level Three—principal

The Levels of Communication should be explained and shared with your faculty, staff, students, and parents. I also found it very beneficial to include a copy of the communication levels in the faculty handbook and my expectations list. Groups such as PTAs/PTOs, volunteers, and school partners also need to be made aware of the communication network in your school. There will be a small percent of your parent body and community who will feel more comfortable with consulting individuals who are not directly involved with their child. Do not let this fact immobilize you. Accept it and take advantage of the influence other key individuals in your school may have with parents and community members. By being what I call ambassadors for the school, you will be able to reach all segments of your community and school population. When members of your various groups are consulted or asked questions by parents or community members who, for whatever reason, are reluctant to approach school personal, the group member will be able to steer them to the first level of communication, the teacher.

Another important area to focus on is communicating with staff, students, central office personnel, local support/service entities, and civic organizations. Is it necessary to have a mechanism in place to establish a communication line with them? Absolutely! Will you have a set time to return telephone calls, see salespeople and vendors, or meet with parents?

I have heard many administrators say they have an open-door policy with their staff, parents, and students. An open-door policy is fine, but there will be times when your door will have to be closed. You will have to block out or schedule times to do the other things pertaining to your principalship. If you don't protect that time, you will have very little time left to do the fun things involved in being the school admin-

istrator. In addition, you will want to establish lines of communication in order to resolve concerns and issues and receive feedback. Listed below are several examples of ways to increase communication among your staff, students, and parents.

Communication Tips

1. Place a suggestion box in the faculty/staff lounges and cafeteria.
2. Require weekly grade-level or team meetings for planning and sharing information.
3. Publish a monthly newsletter or calendar of events for parents, students, and community members.
4. Print a daily bulletin highlighting important reminders or activities for the week.
5. Schedule bimonthly meetings with representatives from your grade levels and special area teachers.
6. Set aside two specific times in your daily schedule that staff members can meet with you as individuals or teams.
7. Meet with your administrative staff prior to the start of each school day to share information and important updates.
8. Greet students and parents daily as they enter and exit your building.

This list is not inclusive. You may use the examples above or replace them with your own ideas to foster communication among key groups and individuals in your school.

The most important time of communication you need to set aside is time for mediation, reflection, prayers, and spiritual growth. No matter what your religious faith or spiritual beliefs are, make time for spiritual rejuvenation. Set your alarm fifteen minutes earlier in the morning and spend that time meditating, reading scriptures, or praying. I found my day always went better when I spent time participating in activities that helped me stay focused and centered. I acknowledged God's control over my life and prayed daily for his strength and guidance before I faced my school day. It is my belief that you start your day on your knees so you can stand tall during the day.

Being a school administrator is a rewarding position where you have the opportunity to touch many lives significantly and make a difference. You will not always have the answers or be sure which way to resolve all situations that arise. God will supply you with the wisdom, patience, and endurance you need to run an effective school. There were many times when I was faced with irate parents or difficult conferences or situations that I had no earthly idea how to solve. The special times I set aside to communicate with God helped me say the right words or remain calm as I listened to parent or staff members' concerns or issues. During my tenure as a school administrator, no one left my conferences shouting or screaming at the top of their lungs. We may not have always agreed, but we always parted on a positive note. I escorted each individual out of my office and wished them a good day. I also encouraged them to contact me in the future if they had any other concerns or questions regarding what we had discussed during our conference. I learned a very important lesson during those trying conferences. Sometimes the success of the conference had more to do with what you did not say than what you did say! Everyone wants to be heard. Take time to listen. Listening is an important component of effective communication.

Creating a Climate for Staff Communication

Bringing a faculty and staff together to achieve common goals and function as a unit is not an easy feat. Every school administrator faces the task of creating a school environment that promotes effective communication and fosters collegiality among faculty and staff. Faculty and staff who feel good about who they are as individuals and professionals will make students and their parents feel good about who they are also.

During my first year as an administrator, I faced quite a different faculty and staff challenge. Assuming the principalship over a school in which I had previously served as an assistant principal put me in the sticky situation of getting established in and assuming responsibility for a different position and role. I

wanted our faculty and staff to gel as a new and unique group even though we had worked together previously.

The first few weeks of school of school were hectic and exciting. My assistant principal and I had worked hard to set the tone for the school year. But after the third week of school, we realized something was missing. The spark was there, but there was no light. On the surface, our staff was polite, cooperative, and pleasant, but we didn't want polite company. We wanted a family unit! We finally realized, during one of our early morning administrative meetings, that we had not quite broken the ice with our staff. How do you suppose we found this out? Well, we just simply asked one of our staff members.

Previously, I mentioned the importance of receiving feedback and input from peer colleagues and trusted mentors. Teachers can also be good barometers for how you are doing. When I asked one of our veteran teachers how we were doing, she was short, sweet, and to the point. "We have a lot of respect for you and our new assistant principal, but we see you as very task oriented. We know you as administrators, but we don't really know you as people."

I thanked her for her candidness and honesty and we pondered the valuable information she had gracefully shared with us. We had spent so much time focusing on the "meat and potatoes" of the school that we had forgotten the "gravy" that would bring things together. Our staff wanted to know us as individuals, and we realized, with the help of the veteran teacher, that we wanted to know our staff also. As a result, I came up with an idea for a faculty and staff activity that would help us "gel" as a staff.

The activity I developed can be done during a faculty meeting and requires very little preparation and limited materials. All you need is a sincere heart, a healthy sense of humor, and a stack of 4" × 6" lined or unlined index cards. I titled the activity "I Have a Secret." The directions for the activity: Ask your staff if they remember seeing the game show in which it was the task of the panel to guess which person was telling the truth about their name and line of work. Tell your staff that they are going to play a similar game, but it will involve guessing secrets.

Distribute the index cards and tell everyone to write down three secrets about themselves that no one knows about. The secrets must be things they do not mind sharing. Allow them ten minutes to write their secrets on the cards. You and your administrative staff should complete index cards as well. Collect the cards and place them in a box or basket. Note: Names are not written on the cards.

Randomly staff members select one card and read the secrets out loud to the group. The object of the activity is for the group to try to guess which staff member's secrets are being read. They have only three opportunities to guess. If there isn't a correct response after three tries, the faculty member who completed the card reveals who she or he is. This activity will be fun as well as surprising! I am happy to report that when we did it, the activity achieved just what we had hoped it would. We had staff members stop us in the hall several weeks after the meeting to ask us questions about the things we had shared.

Do take the time to relax and enjoy each other as professionals as well as people. I will never forget the lesson I learned from that group. You need a balance between task-oriented and human-relation activities. Both are equally important and needed in an effective school.

3

Getting Off on the Right Track

Getting School Started

The big day has finally arrived! All those weeks of planning anxiously during the summer have come to an end. Now it's time to put those plans into action. Preplanning week starts tomorrow, and you are about to face fifty to sixty enthusiastic staff members who are waiting expectantly and eagerly for your leadership. You have established your goals and expectations for the upcoming school year, and now you are charged with the task of gaining the support and commitment of the staff.

The first faculty/staff meeting during preplanning week is going to set the tone for the rest of the school year. As a first-year school administrator, it is going to be extremely important for you to focus on those activities that will get you and the staff organized and prepared for the school year. Do not make the mistake of filling preplanning week with too many meetings. Teachers are more concerned about having quality time in their classrooms to prepare for the bright little eager faces they will meet on the first day of school. In addition to the activities planned at the school level, there will be probably be countywide system-level meetings requiring their attendance also. So, despite the possibility of interruptions during preplanning week, meaningful organizational activities can still help you get the school year off to a good start. The following are items you might consider implementing to help organize your faculty and staff prior to preplanning week. You might also use some of the worksheets I developed throughout the school year as time permits.

Preplanning Organizational Activities

1. Faculty/Staff Handbook
2. Parent/Student Handbook
3. School- and System-Level Committees
4. New Teacher Orientation
5. Welcome Back Letter
6. Open House
7. First Day Plans
8. Opening Exercises
9. Duty Schedules (Arrival and Dismissal)
10. Inclement Weather Plan
11. Schedules (Instructional and Lunch)
12. Lesson Plans (Instructional)
13. Policies and Procedures (School- and System-Level)
14. Classroom Management Plans
15. Bulletin Boards/Display Cases
16. Grade-Level Team/Administrative Meetings
17. Special Programs and Events
18. Extracurricular Activities
19. Parent/Student Conferences
20. Dress Code (Students and Staff)
21. Resource Utilization Approval Form
22. Preplanning Week Schedule
23. Job Responsibilities of Faculty, Staff, and Administrative Staff
24. Expectations for Administration, Faculty, and Staff
25. Components of the Substitute Teacher's Folder

Note: This list is not all inclusive.

Faculty/Staff Handbook

Putting together your first faculty and staff handbook is an excellent opportunity for you to share your vision, goals, and expectations for the school year. If there is a handbook already in place when you arrive, review it from cover to cover. Familiarize yourself with the policies and procedures already place prior to your tenure as principal. During the handbook review process, check off any procedures, policies, or rules that you support or that reflect your leadership style. Note policies or procedures you may want to revise or change. Remember that it is never necessary to reinvent the wheel. Many first-year school administrators make the mistake of coming in and throwing out or discrediting everything that was put in place before their arrival. It's better to use that first year as a year for growing. Only change those things that need to be changed. If you do, however, have to make a drastic change, involve the staff as much as possible. Teachers are more likely to take ownership of those things that they are involved with professionally and personally.

Include in your faculty/staff handbook a copy of the school system's job descriptions for each staff member. Following the job descriptions, list your expectations for that particular staff member for the school year. Set aside time during the first general faculty/staff meeting during preplanning to review and discuss your expectations with your staff. Do not forget to include along with your expectations a list of what your staff can expect from you as the school administrator and instructional leader in the school.

Parent/Student Handbook

The main focus of your parent/student handbook is to provide parents and students with school and system policies and procedures. You may also include school goals and your vision in the parent/student handbook. Many school systems have certain school board policies that must be placed in the handbook. If a parent/student handbook is not available at your school, contact your district's central administrative office and request a copy. Most handbooks include the following: student dress code, arrival/dismissal times, attendance, discipline policies, school-level rules, promotion/retention policy, report card dates, school calendar, information about Parent and Teacher Associations or Parent and Teacher Organizations, procedures for visitors on school campus, scheduling parent conferences, and other pertinent information.

School- and System-Level Committees

Every year school systems adopt or review curricular textbooks and materials. Contact the appropriate central office administrator to find out system-level committees needing a school-level representative from your school. Make a list of those committees and find out the names of last year's committee members from your school. Try to contact these individuals over the summer or prior to the end of the school year to determine whether or not they are interested in serving again as the school-level representative.

Using last year's committee members will allow you time to get to know the current individual and other staff members. If the current individual is no longer interested in serving in the same capacity for another year, respect their decision and ask them if there is another staff member they could recommend to take their place who would represent the school as well as they did. Contact the recommended individual and let them know you got their name from a colleague who felt they would be an excellent replacement. Generally, teachers are very willing to participate on system-level committees and feel honored being selected to represent the school.

Participating in system-level committees provides teachers with the opportunity to work with teachers from other schools on their grade level and gives them a broader perspective of the curriculum. Also, teachers gain new insight and understandings through the dialogue among other colleagues and consultants.

Keep a copy of your system-level committee members and change the members on a regular basis. Frequently, as school administrators, we continue to assign the same individuals to different committees. Remember that part of your responsibility as the instructional leader in the school is to provide opportunities for growth for your entire staff. It is very true that everyone will be at different levels and stages of professional development.

Teachers will never grow and mature professionally if you do not take the time to allow them to grow. Teachers who are used constantly will eventually "burn out" and lose their natural enthusiasm. Rotate committee membership while motivation and enthusiasm are high. Follow the same procedure when selecting committee members for your school-level committees. Some school-level committees you might consider creating are: Safety Committee, Parent/School Advisory Committee, Social Committee, School Fund-Raising Committee, Curriculum Committee, Parent Involvement Committee, PTA/PTO Committee, and Special Programs/Events Committee.

New Teacher Orientation

New staff members have different concerns and needs than returning veteran or experienced teachers. Set aside a day prior to preplanning to orient your new staff members. Allowing the teachers the opportunity to meet as a group gives them the time to meet informally with you and other new members of your staff.

New teachers should be given a copy of the faculty/staff and the parent/student handbooks for review. Provide a tour of the building and show them where their classrooms are located. Assign new teachers a returning teacher as a "buddy" for the school year. If possible, assign the new teacher to an individual who was new the previous school year. From experience, I have learned that new staff members feel more comfortable asking questions from individuals who were in the same shoes the previous year. Grade-level chairpersons or team leaders also make excellent buddies.

To keep my new teacher orientation sessions up to date and meaningful, I used ideas from the current new teachers to plan orientation sessions for the next school year. Also, I had current new teachers take part in the orientation session. Use your new teacher orientation session as a time for your new staff to get to know you and for you to get to know them. Always be open to suggestions to improve your sessions.

Welcome Back Letter

Two weeks before it is time for the faculty and staff to report back to work, write a brief letter welcoming them back to work. Include in the letter a schedule for preplanning week. It is also nice to write something about yourself. Make sure you let them know how much you are looking forward to working with them in the upcoming school year. Add a nice homey touch by enclosing a picture of you and your family. Also, invite them to drop by and meet you prior to the opening of school. Be sure to let them know what time of day you will be available for visits.

Open House

The first day of school by nature can be very hectic for faculty, staff, students, and parents. You can eliminate some of the nervous anxiety of students and parents by having an open house before the first day of school. Our school system has set aside the day before school as open house countywide for our elementary and middle schools.

Parents and students get the opportunity to meet their teachers, visit the classrooms, and tour the building. Classroom rosters are posted in the cafeteria or placed on bulletin boards. Faculty and staff members are available to answer questions and direct parents to different areas in the buildings. This also provides teachers an opportunity to present to parents and students their expectations, class rules, and class goals for the school year. Many of my teachers used this time to have parents sign up to be room parents and volunteers or to schedule get-acquainted conferences.

First Day Plans

The first day of school can be very hectic and chaotic without plans to head off opening day jitters. Try to prepare your school and staff as much as possible for those events that can be foreseen to take place regardless of the situation. Enlist and utilize the assistance of all staff and faculty members.

Staff your office with additional help to answer new parent questions and escort students to classrooms. Run extra copies of class rosters and post teachers and staff members strategically in the building to assist lost or wandering parents and students. Copies of each teacher's class roster need to be placed outside their classroom door. Everyone in the building should wear nametags for identification.

While parents of entering students were completing enrollment forms in our front office area, new students were escorted to the media center to wait for new classroom assignments or placement testing. The media specialist and media clerk read stories to the children and showed filmstrips or videotapes. School maps were also provided to help familiarize parents with the building. Extra copies of the bus and lunch schedules were made available for new parents as well. School calendars were distributed to provide parents with information regarding holidays and report card dates.

Schedule a brief faculty meeting the last pre-planning day to ensure that everyone is aware of the plans for the first day of school. Everyone needs to be ready to respond to questions asked by a wandering parent or student. There will be some things that will happen that you cannot foresee or plan for, but do not concern yourself with wondering about those things. Plan for those things that you know will happen.

Opening Exercises

The procedure you follow to start the school day will set the tone for the entire instructional day and the rest of the school year. Most schools start their day with reciting the Pledge of Allegiance, singing a patriotic song, a thought for the day, and announcements. In the state of Georgia, we are required to have a moment of silence as a part of our opening exercises.

Regardless of what school systems require as a part of the opening exercises, it is a good idea to have school-wide procedures to ensure continuity and consistency. Involve the students by delegating the responsibility for leading the Pledge of Allegiance to different grade levels at different times. Start the year off giving the responsibility to the upper grade level in your school. Classes take turns weekly, so the lower grades will participate later as the school year unfolds. A taped patriotic song can be played over the school's public address system. This is an activity that the children enjoy and take pride in doing for the school. Following is a sample Pledge of Allegiance form that may be used or revised to meet your staff needs.

Worksheet #12

Pledge of Allegiance Schedule

Fifth Grade

Teacher_____

Teacher_____

Teacher_____

Teacher_____

Fourth Grade

Teacher_____

Teacher_____

Teacher_____

Teacher_____

Third Grade

Teacher_____

Teacher_____

Teacher_____

Teacher_____

Week

Week of_____

Week of_____

Week of_____

Week of_____

Week of_____

Week of_____

Week of_____

Week of_____

Week of_____

Week of_____

Week of_____

Week of_____

Worksheet #12 (*continued*)

Second Grade

Teacher_____

Teacher_____

Teacher_____

Teacher_____

First Grade

Teacher_____

Teacher_____

Teacher_____

Teacher_____

Kindergarten

Teacher_____

Teacher_____

Teacher_____

Teacher_____

Week

Week of_____

Week of_____

Week of_____

Week of_____

Week of_____

Week of_____

Week of_____

Week of_____

Week of_____

Week of_____

Week of_____

Week of_____

Note: Individuals or small groups of students may lead the opening exercises.

Arrival and Dismissal Procedures

Organizing the traffic flow in your building is key to obtaining a smooth transition as students arrive and exit the building. To help you design a procedure for arrival and dismissal, if it is possible, observe the school prior to the beginning of your principalship before summer vacation. Review the plan that is already in existence. Ask yourself the following questions: Does the traffic seem to flow smoothly? Are there any bottlenecks? Are there any areas that need hall monitors to guide students to their classrooms? Do you need to use all entrances and exits in your building? Are the drop-off and pick-up areas for students located strategically?

Develop a duty schedule for arrival and dismissal with staff input. Be aware that most teachers do not like to perform this duty. However, I found the best arrival and dismissal procedure plan is one that is developed by the staff. Assign each grade level the responsibility of providing a plan to dismiss students who walk, ride the bus, or are transported home by their parents. Individual plans should be consolidated into one plan agreed upon by all grade levels. Review the plan submitted by your staff carefully. Implement the arrival and dismissal procedures and observe the plan in action the first several weeks of school. Make changes as needed throughout the school year. Distribute copies of the arrival and dismissal schedule to your office staff as well as to other key individuals in the school. Be prepared to provide coverage in the event of absences or illnesses.

Inclement Weather Plan

What do you do when there is a threat of a tornado, hurricane, or severe thunderstorms? Does your school system have a policy and procedure to follow in the event of early school closings because of bad weather? Rainy day plans are necessary. Many school systems contact local radio and television stations to inform parents of school closings. Make sure your procedures for inclement weather and emergency closings are published in your parent/student handbook. Your teachers may provide valuable input in de-

veloping an inclement weather or emergency plan. Once a plan is in place, feel free to modify it based on needs that are identified during actual inclement weather or emergency situations. When formulating an inclement weather plan, consider the following:

1. Do you want to hold students in each teacher's classroom?
2. Do you want all of the teachers and students to report to a central location in the event of inclement weather?
3. How will you handle neighbors or friends picking up students?
4. What adjustments will need to be made to manage additional traffic?
5. How will you contact parents to let them know school buses will be late in departing?

In times of bad weather and emergencies, students, parents, and staff members are anxious and may not behave as expected. Train your staff to be calm, patient, and understanding. Use your auxiliary staff and teachers to assist the office staff with responding to anxious parents and frantic telephone calls. Everyone needs to realize that parents are concerned about the safety and well-being of their children just as you are. Demonstrate your concern and care and respond in a positive manner regardless of the situation or circumstance.

Schedules and Lesson Plans

Schedules and lesson plans are the backbones of the total school program. Putting together an effective schedule can facilitate or hinder the instructional activities and services provided for children. Lesson plans serve as a guide or a road map to get your school and students to where you want them to be.

I am a firm believer in not reinventing the wheel. If schedules are already in place, as a first-year school administrator, you should use the current school schedules and modify them throughout the year if necessary.

I have used grade-level teams and special area teachers to suggest times to provide special area classes like music, art, physical education, and special education. Once teachers are given a master schedule plan, they meet as teams with special area teachers to plan the schedule for the school year. This team planning may take place during preplanning your first year as principal, but after that, planning for the upcoming school year should take place during the latter part of the school year or during postplanning.

Lesson plans should consist of components that will enable you to monitor the instructional program and chart the progress of the teachers on school- and system-level objectives. Teachers' lesson plans must provide clear instructions and outline specifically what is planned for students. Basic components of the lesson plans should include the following: objectives, procedures, materials, and evaluation. Many school systems and administrators require teachers to provide documentation to support instruction on specific norm-reference test objectives and curriculum objectives. Find out what your school system requires. Provide teachers with a list of the basic components you want present in their lesson plans. It is also helpful to provide teachers with sample lesson plans that meet your expectations.

I did not request lesson plans from my staff the first week of school. Teachers were encouraged to come up with their own lesson plan format that incorporated the basic components I specified. These lesson plan formats were reviewed and approved by the administrative staff. Emergency lesson plans to cover three days were submitted by the teachers and kept on file in my office. Emergency plans were helpful in the event a teacher had to be out unexpectedly.

Clear and simple instructions were left for substitutes as well. A substitute folder containing the following information was placed on each teacher's desk for the substitute's use.

Components of the Substitute Teacher's Folder

1. Class seating chart
2. Instructional schedule
3. Arrival and dismissal duty schedule
4. Names of students who attended special needs classes and times they were scheduled
5. A list of students' home and emergency telephone numbers
6. Substitute teacher's evaluation form
7. Lunch/physical ed./music schedules
8. A map of the school
9. Faculty and parent/student handbooks
10. A list identifying which students ride the bus, walk home, or are transported by parents
11. A copy of the teacher's classroom management plan and class rules
12. A list of special programs or events
13. The name of a "buddy" teacher
14. Pledge of Allegiance schedule

Administrative Policies and Procedures

Teachers and staff members need to be familiar with policies and procedures that directly and indirectly impact students and parents. From time to time, teachers will either be asked questions or faced with decisions concerning attendance, grades, student behavior, promotion, and retention. Your staff's familiarity with system- and school-level administrative policies and procedures will help lighten the school administrator's load.

Carefully review your system's administrative manual and list all of the policies and procedures related to the aforementioned areas that you want your staff to be aware of. (Note: There may be additional areas you want to include that are not identified in the administrative manual.) After the list is compiled with appropriate page numbers referenced, place it in the faculty/staff handbook. Review this page with your faculty and staff during preplanning week. As administrative policies and procedures are updated and revised, replace the old copies with the revised policies and procedures. The same procedure can be used with those policies and procedures that are implemented at the school level.

If you decide to incorporate the levels of communication discussed previously in this handbook, placing the procedure in your parent/student handbook is a way to communicate to all parents the procedures or steps to follow if there is a question or concern regarding their child or the school.

I found that a section in the handbook devoted to in-house forms used for requesting sick leave, personal days, professional leave, field trips, discipline referrals, classroom maintenance requests, and other pertinent items was very helpful. Along with the samples of forms, I also specified which office staff individuals were to receive which forms and the deadline for submitting the forms, if appropriate. To keep your office staff from being bombarded daily by requests for forms, place the forms in the teachers' lounge in a file cabinet for easy access. The office staff should periodically check the file to ensure there are always forms available.

It is helpful to put forms needed for your office records on NCR paper. I had discipline referrals, midterm progress reports, bus referrals, and parent conference forms put on NCR paper. By doing so, we were able to have copies for teachers and parents. Placing certain forms on NCR paper minimizes the cost of running copies for distribution to teachers, staff, and other appropriate central office personnel.

Classroom Behavior Management Plan

Classroom management and student discipline are major concerns for teachers and school administrators. If there is no classroom control and student discipline, learning cannot take place. Teachers will spend precious instructional time trying to gain control of their classrooms, and you, as the administrator, will spend the majority of your time seeing students in your office.

Students as well as parents need to know what is expected of them. Regardless of the grade level, students need a framework to help them develop self-discipline and appropriate behavior. They also need to have clear consequences for inappropriate behavior and know what those consequences are.

I believe classroom management and student discipline begins at the classroom level with support from the administrative level. Teachers who send students to the office constantly are sending a pointed message to their students: "I cannot handle your behavior, and I am letting someone else handle you."

Provide teachers with resources and assistance to help them set up their classroom discipline plan. Effective classroom management plans consist of class rules and clear consequences for appropriate and inappropriate behavior. Sending children to the office is a strategy that should be reserved for serious offenses. The school administrator should review and approve each teacher's classroom management plan. Copies of the plan should be kept on file in the office and given to parents. Teachers can schedule parent conferences, during which they review their classroom management plans with parents. The administrative office and parents should receive an updated copy of the classroom management plan if changes are made to it.

The classroom management plans may be developed individually or as a team. Many teachers like to develop grade-level plans to promote consistency across a grade level. Behavior expectations should also be formulated for the cafeteria, halls, and assemblies. These expectations of behavior should be posted in key areas around the building and published in the faculty and parent/student handbooks.

Remember, the more able your teachers are to handle discipline at the classroom level, the more time you will have to function as the instructional leader of the school. Teachers who do not handle any of their disciplinary problems will become totally dependent on you and others to solve their classroom management problems. Provide staff development training for individuals who may be weak in the area of student discipline and classroom management. There are many excellent assertive discipline programs and classroom management materials available for classroom teachers.

Bulletin Boards/Display
Cases Decorating Schedule

Keeping hall bulletin boards and display cases decorated can be made easy as a shared responsibility in your school. Develop a monthly schedule and let each grade level select a month to decorate a selected hall bulletin board display case. The bulletin board and display case schedule should be given to your staff during pre-planning week. Encourage the teachers to show-case their students' work. Teachers can also use the hallways to display special student projects and other activities. Parents and students alike enjoy viewing student work.

You may also assign the Parent and Teacher Association/Parent and Teacher Organization a display case or bulletin board to provide information about the activities and functions they are involved in for the school.

Grade-Level Team Meetings

Decide how you want to organize your faculty and staff to disseminate information and receive input and feedback about the day-to-day operations of your school. I found it very effective to have a committee representing the different grade levels and special areas to plan upcoming events and share information discussed at monthly administrative meetings. Additionally, team meetings can serve as a forum to discuss grade-level or school-wide issues or concerns. Try to involve your staff whenever possible in the decision-making process. Encourage your faculty and staff to generate possible solutions to problems presented at team meetings.

Special Programs, Events, and Extracurricular Activities

Review a handbook from the previous school year to find out if there are any programs or events that are traditional events for the school. It is better to try to continue the programs, events, and special activities that have been already established by your predecessor. Use your first year as the new administrator to evaluate the effectiveness of the current programs, events, and extracurricular activities. If changes need to be made, involve your faculty, staff, students, and parents. Always be open to suggestions and solicit assistance from faculty, staff, parent volunteers, and school partners. The success of any program, activity, or event depends on the commitment, support, and interest of the people involved.

The areas briefly discussed in this section are not all inclusive. I offer them merely as suggestions, because I found them to be very helpful for me as I started the school year. In my estimation, the most important aspect is taking the time to plan and put in writing those things you would like to see take place in your school. Remember Rome was not built in a day. Use each day and every school year as a building block. The road to school effectiveness is challenging and continuous. Planning helps you to focus on school needs and goals.

4

Parent and Student Involvement Strategies and Techniques

Parent involvement in their children's education is a key factor in helping children gain higher test scores and achievement. Parents who spend time working with their child obtain an understanding of their child's intellectual, social, emotional, and physical development. Many schools, however, indicate great difficulty in getting their parents involved with the school and their child's education.

Many parents work and cannot afford the luxury of taking time off work to come to school. Some parents feel intimidated by school personnel and are reluctant to have contact with them. Also, in some instances, parents have had bad experiences with school as a child and color their perceptions of school with those early experiences. Other parents may be young, single parents who do not have any idea how to get involved with the school or know how to help their child with homework at home.

We, as educators, must make every effort to involve parents with their child's educational development. It is a challenge that will help all parties concerned in the long run. If we are going to have any impact in the lives of our students, we must develop programs and strategies to bring our parents back to schools.

I want to share with you some programs and activities I formulated and used during my tenure as an elementary school administrator. None of the activities guarantee success, but I feel it is important and necessary to try as many different activities as you can implement effectively. You will find that different parents will respond to different types of programs or activities. Those activities that seem to generate a lot of interest and participation among parents should be extended and continued. Refine and continue to develop activities that generate a moderate amount of interest or participation. Do not be afraid to take a risk and try something

new. You may be surprised by the reception your new idea receives. Involving students and their parents together in activities is a surefire way to get parents to participate in school-related activities and programs. Try to meet the different needs of your school's parent clientele by planning activities and programs that will enable maximum participation and involvement. We must, as school administrators, be willing to creatively use our time and resources to accommodate various parent schedules.

I am briefly discussing and sharing with you activities, programs, and strategies I used to involve parents and students. All these activities may be modified to meet the needs of individual schools or school systems.

Get-Acquainted Conferences

This a good parent activity to conduct during the beginning of the school and throughout the school year as new students and their parents enroll in your school. Parents are children's first teachers. There are many special things they can share with their child's teacher to help foster a good working relationship between the school and home. Teachers are encouraged to schedule what I call a get-acquainted conference with the parent of each student in their class. The purpose of the conference is to meet informally with each student's parents and get to know the student as well as the students' parents. Teachers may also use this time to share information about their class expectations and goals for the school year. Set aside the first two or three weeks of school to hold the get-acquainted conferences. Parents can be asked to complete Worksheet #13 before their scheduled get-acquainted conference. I found the worksheet to be an effective icebreaker for the conferences.

Worksheet #13

Get-Acquainted Conference

My Child Is Special

Child's Name _____

Nickname _____(if applicable)

1. My child's favorite free time activity is_____

2. My child's hobbies are_____

3. My child's interests are_____

4. My child enjoys learning about_____

5. My child is special because_____

Write below what you feel are your child's strengths.

_____

_____

_____

_____

Write below the types of activities you feel will help your child enjoy learning.

_____

_____

_____

_____

Parent Volunteers

Getting parents to work in the classrooms is an effective way to encourage participation in the educational activities of the school. It also provides an opportunity for parents to learn more about the school and the curriculum. I have seen parents who were first very critical of a school and its policies become staunch supporters once they began volunteering in a school.

An effective volunteer program will have specific guidelines and objectives. Parents can serve as resource persons and share their expertise, talents, and experiences with students to help enrich the educational experiences of students.

Before a parent volunteer program is developed and implemented, conduct a meeting or survey your faculty and staff to determine the volunteer needs of the school. It is also important to select an administrator or teacher to coordinate the parent volunteer program in your building.

If a volunteer program is already in place, find out how the program operated and who coordinated the activities. Many school systems have a community/school partnership involvement policy. Make sure you review your system's policy before you try to set up a volunteer program. Conduct a needs assessment to determine the effectiveness of the existing volunteer program. Feedback received can be used to improve the existing volunteer program in your school. Remember, maintain those things that work and refine or modify those areas needing improvement. Use the following questions and worksheets to serve as a guide to help you formulate an effective volunteer program in your school.

1. What will your role be as the principal in the parent volunteer program?
2. What are the goals of your parent volunteer program?
3. How will parents serve your school?
4. Will you limit your volunteers to parents only?
5. Will you include school partners or community volunteers also?
6. Will you conduct a parent or community volunteer orientation session?
7. Will you have specific rules and procedures for volunteers to follow?
8. Will the volunteer program operate throughout the week or only on certain days of the week?

Once you have responded to the above questions, establish a parent volunteer committee consisting of teacher representatives and other interested individuals. This committee should meet with your guidance to develop a staff survey or other needs-assessment instruments to decide which volunteer services could be used by your staff. Services that can be provided by volunteers in your school are as follows:

1. Serve as a resource person for the school.
2. Serve as a tutor for reading, mathematics, and other subject areas.
3. Make games and other instructional materials for teachers.
4. Serve as an assistant in the media center.
5. Serve as an office helper or clerical assistant.
6. Provide childcare services for parents attending school-sponsored workshops and parent sessions.
7. Serve as a bus monitor on class or school field trips.
8. Serve as a demonstrator for art and other class projects.
9. Serve as a safety monitor and school crossing guard.
10. Serve as a playground monitor.
11. Serve as a class pen pal.
12. Serve as a volunteer computer instructor or assistant.
13. Serve as a guest speaker for specific careers and topics.
14. Serve as a breakfast and lunchroom monitor.
15. Serve as a room parent for a class.
16. Serve as a class storyteller or reader.

Use the Teacher Needs Assessment Survey (Worksheet #14) to determine specific needs of each teacher on your staff. Make sure you include special area teachers, such as music, art, and physical education. Many times we forget to include them, although they enjoy parent participation and often have activities parents can assist them with throughout the school year.

Worksheet #14

Teacher Needs Assessment Survey

Teacher's Name_____   Grade/Subject_____

Directions: Listed below are some activities a volunteer might assist you with. Indicate area(s) of interest to you and return the completed form to the parent volunteer coordinator by _____.

_____Tutoring students
    ____Reading
    ____Mathematics
    ____Language Arts
    ____Science
    ____Social Studies
    ____Other_____

_____Resource Speaker
    Area of Expertise _____

_____Careers
    Area of Expertise_____

_____Teacher Assistance
    ____Bulletin Boards
    ____Art Activities
    ____Clerical
    ____Other_____

_____Field Trips

Worksheet #14 (*continued*)

_____Lunchroom or Breakfast Monitor

_____Reading to the Class

_____Making Games and Instructional Materials

_____Classroom Mother or Father

_____Computer Instruction

_____Copying Instructional Material

_____Other_____

I would like a volunteer to work with me the following days and times:

Day(s) of the week	*Times*
_____	_____
_____	_____

I would like the following activities/tasks completed at home by parents who are unable to volunteer during the day:

_____

_____

_____

I am interested in having volunteers in my classroom that possess the following skills/interests:

_____

_____

_____

Worksheet #15

Sample School Volunteer Skills and Interest Survey

Dear _____   Date _____

    Thank you for your interest in serving as a volunteer at our school. We match our school volunteers and classrooms based on volunteer skills and the interests and needs of each teacher. Your assistance is needed with this process. Please fill in the information below and return the completed survey to our school volunteer coordinator by _____.

I am interested in providing assistance as a

____Tutor

____Resource Person

____Storyteller

____Computer Assistant

____Clerk

____Room Parent

____Lunchroom/Breakfast Monitor

____Traffic Monitor

____Reader

____Bus Monitor

____Field Trip Chaperone

____Media Center Assistant

____Maker of Instructional Materials

____Arts and Crafts Instructor

____Other

_____

_____

_____

Worksheet #15 (*continued*)

List below specific skills you would like to share with a class or the school.

_____

_____

_____

List below specific interests you would like to share with a class or the school.

_____

_____

_____

_____

What days and times are you able to volunteer your services?

                  Day(s)   *Time(s)*

_____

_____

_____

_____

Worksheet #16

Volunteer Assignment Sheet

Name of Volunteer _____   Date _____

Assigned Teacher _____

Day(s) and Time(s) of Volunteering

_____

_____

_____

_____

_____

Volunteer Assignment(s)

1. _____

2. _____

3. _____

4. _____

5. _____

Parents Active in Learning with Students (PALS)

During my years as a Title I Reading Teacher for the Camden City Public School System in Camden, New Jersey, I encouraged parents to help their children improve their reading skills by participating in PALS. Instructional games and materials were provided for parents to assist with sight word drills, vocabulary development, and reading comprehension.

Parents as well as interested community volunteers were shown how to use teacher-made instructional materials I designed and a variety of techniques to use to help their children decode words and improve comprehension. Each person was assigned a Title I student to work with during a twenty-to-thirty-minute session in the classroom. PALS also listened to children read outside the classroom in the hallway. I believe the parent and community volunteers had more fun than the students did!

This idea can be used for other subject areas. Parents and community volunteers gain a better understanding of the learning process and school's curriculum through the eyes of children. Several volunteers were able to motivate and spark a renewed interest in reading among my students and their own children as a result of their enthusiasm and interest.

Coffee or Tea with Me

A first-year school administrator spends the entire school year getting to know their staff, students, parents, and community. It is, however, important for your staff, students, and parents to know you as well. Staff members and students have a better opportunity to know you than parents or community members.

A strategy or technique I used to give parents the opportunity to know me as an individual and administrator was to invite them to meet me. I set aside time in the morning and afternoon to chat with parents who expressed an interest in meeting with me. A letter was sent home explaining the purpose of "Coffee or Tea with Me" sessions. I met informally with parents and provided light refreshments, including coffee, tea, and juice. Parents also used our sessions to ask questions about the curriculum and other general instructional matters or concerns. These informal sessions provided me with an avenue to share and discuss our school's short- and long-range goals. Our perspectives were broadened as a result of the interchange of ideas and philosophies during the sessions. I cannot think of a better way to receive feedback and input from parents and community members. Also, in some instances, parents felt less intimidated or fearful about coming to the school or meeting with school administrators and teachers. So, as you can see, a little coffee or tea can go a long way!

Ice Cream Social or Bake Sale

Having an ice cream social or bake sale is a fun way to raise money for instructional materials and improve home/school and teacher relations. At the cost of a $1.00 per child, parents were invited to come back one evening and enjoy ice cream and cake as a family. We played soothing music over our public address system while parents heard about the learning activities their children will be participating in during the school year. We set aside two evenings for the ice cream socials. Parents of kindergarten, first, and second grade students met on the first night, and third, fourth, and fifth grade students and parents gathered together on the second night.

The ice cream social was a big success! We had the opportunity to see parent-child interactions in a relaxed and informal setting. Parents were able to interact with the staff in an informal setting as well. The teachers and I served our parents and students ice cream and cake as they went through our serving line.

Random Calls of Parent Contact

There is an old saying that "no news is good news." A good school administrator who wants to stay in touch with his or her clientele will always seek to gain feedback from parents. A strategy that works well and builds good lines of communication between the home and school is planned random telephone calls to parents and/or community members.

Select a specific time during the day or afternoon to telephone parents in a specific grade level. You do not have to spend a long time talking with parents during these calls. Remember parents have days that are as busy as some of your days! Take a few minutes to ask how their son or daughter is doing in school. Are they pleased with their child's progress? Do they have any questions about the curriculum or school policies? Do they have any suggestions to help make the school more responsive to their or their children's needs? Are there any areas we need to improve?

I found these telephone calls to be informative and fun. Parents enjoy hearing from you and love the opportunity to provide feedback. Sometimes we get a narrow view of how we are doing as an administrator and school because we only have contact from a few parents. Broaden your perspective and communication base through telephone calls.

Also, you may use these telephone calls to share good news about their children. Some parents only hear from us when their children are not behaving their best. Involve your staff by asking teachers to share good news about students in their classes with you. To personalize your call and give parents a "warm fuzzy," share the good news you learned with the parents. You will not only make a parent's day, but you will also strengthen communication between school and home.

Parent Newsletter and Calendar of Events

A well-informed parent will be a more involved parent. With the assistance of your staff and Parent and Teacher Association, keep your parents abreast of school news and activities. A newsletter might be published once a month. Important items such as meetings, field trips, or special programs can be included in the newsletter. You can also include tips to help parents work with their children at home and other curriculum-related areas. Also, set aside a column to explain a specific area of curriculum or a new program.

Create a calendar of events that can be placed on the refrigerator to help parents remember important events or dates, such as school vacations and report card dates. This too can be a joint project of the school and Parent and Teacher Association. Also, take the time to send copies of your newsletter and calendar of events to community members, school partners, and local businesses. The more aware your community is of what you are doing, the better support you will build for your school.

Breakfast or Lunch with the Principal

Parents and students enjoyed this activity immensely! Once or twice a month, invite parents who are able to make arrangements to have breakfast or lunch with you. This will give you the opportunity to showcase your breakfast and lunch program as well as highlight some of the activities of your school. I always include, if time permits, a tour of the school. Many of your community members and school partners are interested in seeing firsthand what is going on in a school. Smiling faces and happy students are the best salespersons for winning support of your school's instructional program and goals. Also use this time to answer any questions or concerns that may be expressed by your guests.

Having breakfast or lunch with my students was one of the most rewarding activities of my day. Students ate with me as a reward for academic achievement or appropriate behavior. Generally, however, I randomly selected students from different grade levels to join me during breakfast or lunch. This was my special time to talk with students about school and their experiences in general. Students give you another perspective on what is happening in your school. Remember, your student body is directly impacted by programs and activities planned or developed by your staff to meet school goals. Their feedback and input is meaningful as well as beneficial. Take time out of your busy day to communicate and have contact with your most important customers or consumers—your students.

Breakfast with Santa

Here's a neat idea to tie in with the holiday season! One of my second grade teachers approached me with an idea for an activity for December—Breakfast with Santa. I thought it was a super way to spread holiday cheer among our students and school family. We put our heads together and came up with a plan that involved interested members of my staff. You would be amazed at the different talents and abilities you have at your fingertips.

We had a parent volunteer dress up as Santa Claus and decorated the stage with a home Christmas scene. This served as our backdrop for pictures with Santa Claus after a hearty breakfast. At the cost of a $1.00 per student, students could have Polaroid pictures taken with Santa that were placed in picture frames designed by a staff member. The school cafeteria was turned into a Christmas wonderland with holiday songs playing as parents and children enjoyed their breakfast. Santa walked around the tables distributing candy canes and chatting with the children and their families. Staff members served the breakfast and also circulated among the families.

This activity was a pleasant Saturday morning activity for all of us. I cannot think of a better way to greet the holiday season and welcome in the New Year. School funds were used to pay for the cost of the breakfast and salaries of the cafeteria staff who prepared the breakfast for us. You and your staff may want to incorporate this idea and plan other activities to build rapport and promote community spirit among your staff, students, and parents.

Grandparent Rockers and Readers

Good school administrators try to use all the resources available in the school and surrounding community. Senior citizens are an excellent, though underutilized, resource. There are many capable and skilled mature individuals who enjoy working with children. Have you ever thought about asking grandparents to read to children in your school?

Invite grandparents or senior citizens to serve as volunteer readers for your school. Obtain a rocking chair for each classroom or place a rocking chair in your media center for the volunteers to sit on as they read. The grandparents and children will just love it. The elementary school where I served as the principal was next to the Kings Bay Naval Base in St. Marys, Georgia. Many of the children's grandparents lived in different areas of the United States. Other grandparent or senior citizen volunteers can serve as surrogate grandparents for such students. Try this activity in your school. I am certain involving grandparents or senior citizens will be beneficial to your entire staff and student body.

Appreciation Tea

Pay tribute to all of your parent and community volunteers by holding a special ceremony in their honor. You may also recognize your Parent and Teacher Association officers at this time. The first appreciation tea I held was conducted in our school's cafeteria. Staff members helped us provide refreshments by bringing their favorite covered dish.

Invitations were sent to volunteers as well as room parents. The response to the first appreciation tea was overwhelming. We had a brief program and provided every volunteer with a certificate of appreciation.

We also invited central office staff and resource people who had assisted our staff throughout the school year. Teachers and other staff members got a kick out of sharing their culinary delights with our parents and community. Students can be involved as greeters and servers. We also had different grade levels make placemats and decorations for the cafeteria. This is also a perfect opportunity to showcase student work or class projects. Students can also open the festivities with a heartfelt welcome and pleasant greeting. Let your imagination run away with you! This type of activity can be used to recognize students and staff as well.

Career Day

Add a twist to Halloween! Instead of staff and students dressing up as their favorite monster, creature, or character, have them dress as the person representing their career of the future. Your staff and students will get a kick out of trying to guess each other's career costume. Also, this activity can be related to different units of study. I cannot think of a better way to introduce children to the different careers that are available to them.

Prizes may be awarded for the most creative costume in each classroom. Involve community members by having them judge the costumes for the event. Don't forget to contact your local newspaper reporters to publicize the festivities!

Staff and Student Warm Fuzzies

Build staff and student morale and nurture a positive school climate by dispensing "warm fuzzies" among your staff and student body. Armed with a pack of 3" x 5" index cards and a pen, you can capture and reinforce acts of kindness and appropriate behavior in your school. You will find that staff members will enjoy the recognition as much as or more than the students.

I would write a brief note on the card, recognizing what I had observed, attach a peppermint or miniature candy bar to the card, and place it in their mailbox. Students were invited to make a special trip to my office and make a selection from a bag of goodies and special treats I kept in a file cabinet drawer.

I would also reward teachers by giving them a coupon card they could redeem after giving me a two- or three-day notice. The coupons had statements such as "You may leave 30 minutes early," "I will read a story to your class for 30 minutes," or "You have a free lunch today." Not only did the staff members enjoy these warm fuzzy coupons, but I also enjoyed my visits in the classrooms. As you can see, I benefited from the warm fuzzies too.

Pat on the Back

Here is another technique to use to recognize staff and students in your school. On the cutout of a hand, write, "You deserve a pat on the back!" Run several copies for distribution to students, staff, and parents. You can also pin the "hand" on their right or left back shoulder. Watch the smiles as they walk through the halls and around the building with their pat on the back.

5

First-Year Lessons

Now that I have had a chance to reflect on my experiences as a first-year school administrator, I am even more grateful to the teachers, students, and parents who were supportive and patient with me during my years as an instructional leader. From time to time, I would share some of my early experiences and episodes with my friends and family. We would laugh about some of the situations I described, which were not funny while they were actually happening. I was often told, however, to write about some of my experiences before I forgot them. I did not write about all of them, but I have a few that I would like to share with you.

Although I did not take the advice of many of my colleagues and friends, I strongly recommend that you keep a notebook and write about your experiences. Your journal of experiences and situations will be a powerful learning tool. You will be amazed at the amount of learning and growth you will gain the first year of your principalship! There are some things that I have a chance to read after a year or two, and it's hard to believe that I was the author of some of the comments and insights. So sit back and enjoy my first-year lessons. I am sure you will have experiences and episodes that will be a source of laughter and joy to you for the rest of your life.

Lesson One—
Tommy and the Fire Ants

The day started out like most days that Monday morning. All was well with the world, and we had started another school day. Nothing out of the unusual happened that might have given me a clue to the upcoming event. As a matter of fact I was feeling rather pleased with myself and very professional.

I wore a new dress purchased over the weekend and a pair of high heels as I went about my "principal" duties for the day. Now that I have had a chance to think about that day, I know it was a very bad idea to wear those heels! I had no idea what was in store for me.

Crooked River Elementary School is near the Kings Bay Naval Base off of a busy thoroughfare called Spur 40. The school was just a little over a year old, and there were no sidewalks leading away from the school property. The Kings Bay Base security gate ran behind and alongside the school property. From the road (Spur 40) to the school's property line is an area of wild weeds, underbrush, palmetto plants, and bushes. To put it simply, woods!

I was on my way back to my office that Monday morning after checking lesson plans when a paraprofessional approached me hurriedly. "Mrs. Hutchinson, Tommy ran out of the building. I think he's running down the road!"

I responded immediately. "Don't worry, I'll go after him. Tell the office what is going on and contact his mother." I shouted these words as I ran out the front door of the building. When I got outside, I spied Tommy walking aimlessly down the road. I was horrified! He could get hit by an oncoming car! I would never been able to live with that for the rest of my life! Tommy was a little kindergartner and new to the school that year. So, I called out to him. He turned around and realized I was coming after him and took off running! Needless to say I took off running after him as fast as I could in my smart new dress and high heel shoes. Oh, did I tell you it happened to be an extremely hot day? So not only was I puffing running after Tommy, but I was also sweating profusely. Thank goodness this happened before I began wearing makeup on a regular basis. Makeup does have the tendency to run when you sweat.

Tommy had no intentions of being caught or making this chase easy for me. I thought maybe since I was the principal he would surely stop running and come back with me without any fuss. Was I ever wrong and idealistic! As I began to close in on Tommy, he looked back and then started running toward the base security gate, which was thankfully away from the road.

Being a good navigator, I quickly turned and followed Tommy through the wooded area in hot pursuit. I finally cornered him near the base gate. I made sure I kept a certain distance from him so my closeness wouldn't cause him to take off running again. Since he had finally stopped running, I decided to try to talk him into coming back to the school with me. Believe me, I said everything I could think of to persuade Tommy to come back with me. It was hot; I was out of breath and sweating profusely. Tommy refused to come back with me. I tried again—at this point I was probably begging him to come back with me. After all, I couldn't leave him out here. Suddenly while I was in the middle of trying to cajole Tommy to come back with me, I noticed a burning sensation on my ankles and feet.

Without looking down, keeping my eyes on Tommy, I slightly bent over and brushed my ankles with my hand. I continued to try to persuade Tommy to come back with me when I noticed that the burning sensation had intensified. This time I did look down at my feet, and to my surprise both feet were covered with red fire ants. I was standing right on top of an ant mound! By this time, ants were traveling up both of my legs. I stepped off of the mound and furiously began to knock the ants off of my legs and feet.

While I was going through my frantic gyrations, Tommy just stood quietly by the fence and watched the spectacle before him. After I had wiped my legs and feet free of the majority of the ants, I resumed my pleading with Tommy. This time after listening to a few more pleas, Tommy took off running as fast as he could. I followed him as he ran through bushes and un-

derbrush along the fence. Suddenly, a woman appeared in front of Tommy and headed him off, and together we were able to catch him. The woman offered to drive us back to the school. I had not realized how far away we were from the building until I looked back.

As Tommy and I climbed into the passerby's car, I thanked her profusely for her help. I explained that I was the new principal at the school and I was trying to catch a runaway student. The woman smiled and said, "I noticed you running after the little boy when I drove by. You looked like you needed some help so I turned around and came back."

So, I returned to the building triumphant, disheveled, sweaty, tired, and itchy. I was teased for several days about my afternoon run. I guess I was a sight to behold when Tommy and I entered the building. It seemed that I spent the rest of the afternoon hitting at ants that seemed to appear from out of nowhere. Of course, this episode was not funny while it was happening, but afterward I began to laugh. I know I must have been a funny sight! I did, however, gain the reputation of someone who would go to extreme efforts to get a job done.

Lessons Learned

I foolishly ran after a runaway student without enlisting the help of other staff members. It was fortunate Tommy did not try to run across the street. I had also misjudged how fast a five-year-old could run! Perhaps my willingness to run after Tommy encouraged him to run farther and faster.

Another lesson I learned from my experience is to be aware of your surroundings and know your elements. Had I watched where I was going I might have been able to avoid the fire ants. Also, I learned that you should not try to solve everything yourself. Your staff is there to assist you; use them and ask for their help. Seeking assistance is not a sign of weakness. Remember that you are only one person. It is teamwork that builds relationships and brings people together. Just think of the chance I took running after Tommy by myself. It was fortunate that the passerby stopped to help me. Do not let foolish pride keep you from seeking advice or help. Your role as a school administrator is not diminished by teamwork.

Lesson Two— Visits from Uncle Murphy

That first year of my principalship, I wanted to show my staff that they had a competent instructional leader. As far as I was concerned, everything had to be perfect. I would take the time to plan and organize things as best I could. I tried to think of every possibility and option to avoid surprises or unnecessary pitfalls.

It seemed that no matter how much planning or time I put into a project or activity, something would come up unexpectedly. I am sure you have heard of Murphy's Law. Well, I believed that Uncle Murphy came to visit at times that we least expected him to! After several frustrating situations, I learned how to handle Uncle Murphy when he paid us a visit.

Lessons Learned

First, nothing is ever perfect. We are all subject to making mistakes regardless of our experiences and training. The best way to handle Uncle Murphy is to be flexible, open, and accepting. Try to have a contingency plan in the event something does not work out as planned. Also, if situations go awry, do not fret. Monitor and adjust. Sometimes those things that go against the original idea are better and more effective.

Second, use the situations or obstacles that arise because of Uncle Murphy as learning experiences. Think of a way to modify a certain project or activity so that it better meets your school's needs. Always strive to improve anything you do. Nothing is ever perfect, and everything can be done differently. Solicit your staff for ideas and feedback. They will give you another perspective and possibly a solution. So, the next time Uncle Murphy comes knocking on your door, welcome him with open arms and a smile!

Lesson Three—The Jamaican Curse

I will probably never forget Danny. He was the cutest and most mischievous little second grader in our school! Danny had transferred to our school from Florida in January. He was an only child and quite spoiled! His mother, who was Jamaican, was stationed at Kings Bay Naval Base.

One day while riding his bicycle home on the bike path from the school to base housing, Danny got into a little scuffle with another second grader from a different classroom. Danny ended up with a few scrapes. I found out about the incident the next day from his upset mother.

We had had a few incidents involving Danny's mother in the past. She believed everyone picked on her child. She did not know that little Danny started many of the altercations with his classmates or school chums. Danny's mother arrived in my office during our second dismissal, very angry and upset. She demanded to see me regarding an incident on the bike path involving her son. My secretary radioed me, and I came into the building from my post outside. The longer you keep angry upset parents waiting, the angrier they get!

As soon as we entered my office and closed the door, Danny's mother demanded that some action be taken against the child who had hurt her son. I calmly told her that I was unaware of the situation and I would investigate the matter and get back with her as soon as I had completed my investigation. She gave me the name of the student who had hurt Danny and agreed to wait until the matter had been investigated. She planned to stop by the next day near dismissal time.

Early the next morning, I investigated the matter and interviewed Danny and the student who had allegedly hurt him on the bike path. I also found two students who had witnessed the incident. During my investigation, I found out that Danny had run into the other student with his bicycle on the path. After the incident, a pushing and shoving match ensued. So, Danny did not quite tell his mother everything that had happened!

True to her word, Danny's mother showed up in the front office right on schedule. After sharing my findings with Danny's mother, she threatened to take matters into her own hands. She was not satisfied with my findings and demanded the address and telephone number of the child who had hurt her son.

Of course, I explained to Danny's mother that I could not provide her with that information. After I refused to comply with her wishes, Danny's mother threatened to put a curse on the other child's family and the school! The only thought that came across my mind was, "It's one thing to have a bad day, but to have someone put a curse on the school because you do not do what they want is quite another thing!" I held my ground. Shortly after that incident, Danny moved to Florida, and I must say we all were a little relieved when he left. Life went on as usual.

Lesson Learned

Stick to your school policies and procedures. Do what is right and fair to all parties concerned. You can never make everyone happy. Be willing to face the consequences of your decisions—both pleasant and unpleasant. Stand behind your principles and do not buckle under threats or curses.

Note: Danny moved back to our school several months later. His mother had a different attitude and was very appreciative of the way we treated her as a parent. Sometimes people have to have other experiences before they can realize the error of their ways.

Lesson Four— The Propane Tank Incident

My tenure as principal was a little unusual. I was the principal at one elementary school twice, so in a sense, I had two first-year experiences. After serving as the assistant principal (one year) and principal (two years), I moved to the central office for two years as a curriculum director. When a principal resigned unexpectedly a week before school was to start, the superintendent sent me back to the school as the interim principal. I re-

mained there as principal for three more years. It was during my second time back that the following incident took place.

As a school administrator I always spent time talking with students during early morning arrival, afternoon dismissals, and lunchtimes. I made it a point to listen to my students. One morning a fourth grade student told one of the assistant principals that he passed by a classmate's house on the way to school. His classmate, who was a fifth grader, had decided he was going to play hooky from school and do something to his fifth grade teacher, who had given him detention earlier that week. He proceeded to tell the fourth grader his plans. The fifth grader was going to set his portable classroom on fire by exploding a propane tank underneath it. The fourth grader told the fifth grader that he was going to school and was not going to play hooky with him. As soon as the fourth grader arrived on campus through the security gate, he told one of the assistant principals what was mentioned to him.

We immediately contacted base security and took other necessary precautions to ensure the safety of the teacher and students in the portable classroom. As a result of our quick action and the tip from the student, the fifth grader was stopped from coming on campus with the propane tank, which was hidden in his book bag. Note: After this episode, the fifth grader was removed from the school and placed in a facility where he would receive specialized counseling.

Lesson Learned

Foster and nurture a school environment that promotes comfortable dialogue between staff, students, and parents. Everyone should feel comfortable conversing with the school administrator and his or her administrative staff. Spend time being visible and talking with students. The biggest lesson I learned from this incident was the importance of listening. I know that from time to time you may hear some wild things from parents, staff, and students. Despite how off-base or out of the way something may sound to you, do investigate. It is better to be safe than sorry.

The incidents I described above are examples of the most memorable lessons I learned as a first-year school administrator. There are many more incidents or situations that contributed to my growth as an administrator. I recommend keeping a daily journal to write down your thoughts, ideas, and reactions to situations throughout the year. At the end of each school year, go back and reread what you have written. Are there any lessons you have learned? Is there anything you will handle differently in the future? You will be amazed at the amount of self-confidence and growth that will unfold before your eyes!

6
Survival Tools for
First-Year School Administrators

Of course, I would be remiss if I did not share with you tools I used as a new school administrator. Writing this handbook has been on my mind for the past four years. I have bits and pieces of notes, ideas, and thoughts I jotted down scattered throughout my office at home in tablets and notebooks. I shared my "pearls of wisdom" with as many new administrators as I could in my school system. I had such a unique and challenging experience during my tenure as a principal that I finally decided to write the handbook and stop talking about it!

What is about to follow is Sheila E's recipe for getting the most out of your first year as an administrator. As I share these tips, you will notice that many of the ideas are not new. But if you are like me, in some respects, there are some things that never really hit home until you are actually experiencing the situation. Once you're involved in the situation or position, the ideas have more meaning and your level of understanding and appreciation increases tremendously.

Delegate

I cannot even count the number of times my educational leadership instructors harped on the importance of delegating. After the first few weeks of school I realized how important delegation is and why it is so important. I started off trying to do everything myself. I did not realize that by doing so I was conveying to my staff that I could do it all and did not need their help. Boy, did I learn fast! An effective school depends on everyone working together as a unit. Use the different talents and abilities of your faculty and staff. Delegate! Delegate! Delegate!

Choose Your Battles

Don't always feel you have to have the upper hand in every situation or incident that occurs. Also, every battle is not worth fighting! Fight only for those things that you have strong beliefs about. For instance, I believe that adults as well as children should be treated with respect. If something occurs that contradicts that belief, I will do anything I can to right the wrong that has been done. Realize that we are all individuals with different backgrounds and experiences. Sometimes you will have to make compromises to achieve what is best for your staff, parents, and students. But never compromise your principles or values! The best resolution to a battle or conflict is when all parties can walk away winners.

Be a Good Listener

I cannot overemphasize the importance of listening. We are, in many instances, so quick to give our advice or make our point that we really do not hear what the other person is saying or not saying. When I tried to listen more and talk less I found some parents, teachers, and students did not necessarily want answers. They just wanted someone to listen and nothing more.

Learn from Mistakes

Do not beat up on yourself when you have found yourself to be in error. You are not expected to be perfect. Admit you made a mistake and do whatever is necessary (if possible) to correct the error. When a mistake occurs, ask yourself what you would do differently if the event happened again. Or, ask yourself what changes need to be made to prevent the situation from occurring in the future. Practice this technique with your staff too. They are human too and will also make mistakes. It is your attitude that determines whether or not they will learn from their mistakes.

Use Stress Busters

I know this is easier sometimes to say than do. Leave your job at work. Spend your hours away from work doing a favorite pastime to relieve stress and anxiety. Whether it's reading, writing, running, walking, or swimming, be sure to implement a regimen you can maintain throughout the school year.

Use Humor

Try to see a funny side in everything that happens! Laughter is another healthy way to relieve stress and tension. I have even resorted to using humor during intense parent conferences as a release valve for all parties concerned. Don't ever take yourself too seriously. If on some days you can't find anything to laugh about, go visit a classroom, read to a class, eat lunch with your students. I guarantee your students will say or do something that will make you laugh.

Create a Warm Fuzzy File

Start your own file of nice notes, letters, and cards you receive from your staff, students, and parents. On rough days, pull out your warm fuzzy file and reread them. This activity will help you refocus on the big picture and dispel those clouds of negativity and self-doubt.

Know Your Customers

Spend time familiarizing yourself with your staff, students, parents, and school commu-

nity. One way to get individuals or people interested in you is to first show interest in them. Having a good understanding of the clientele in your school and community will aid you in meeting the ever-changing needs and interests of your staff, student body, and surrounding community.

Problem-Solving Strategies

There is a great deal of literature available on problem-solving strategies and conflict resolution. I strongly recommend trying different strategies or techniques to deal with situations that may arise throughout the school year. There is never one strategy that will work with every situation. Use a repertoire of problem-solving techniques. Provide training for yourself as well as your staff and student body. The more skilled everyone becomes at resolving conflicts, the less time you will spend mediating between staff, students, and parents.

Know and Like Yourself

This may sound like a strange tool, but it is an extremely important one. The more confident you are about yourself as a person the better school administrator you will be. We all have strengths and areas we would like to improve on. Capitalize on your strengths and sincerely commit to strengthening areas that need improvement. Change is a process and does not happen overnight. If we work at improving, liking, and accepting ourselves everyday, we will make great strides personally and professionally!

Manage Your Time

Have you ever ended the day wondering where the time went and feeling like you accomplished nothing of significance? Before you start taking work home, reevaluate how you spend your time on an average day. Notice if any of the things you do are simply time wasters. Have you delegated responsibilities appropriately? Have you blocked out certain times during the day to do those tasks that require uninterrupted concentration? Is your office staff able to respond to general questions from parents and the public? Do you need to screen your calls during certain times throughout the school day?

Managing your time well is key to getting essential tasks completed. Do not get into the habit of taking things home. Manage your time and you will be able to manage your job.

Remove Albatrosses

Train your staff to solve their own problems. Otherwise, every time something comes up or goes awry, they will look to you to solve the problem. They will bring the problem to you and leave you with the problem or albatross around your neck.

You will hinder the growth of your faculty and staff if you continually come up with solutions to their situations and concerns. Encourage them to present two possible solutions when they request a conference regarding a situation or issue. I found teachers more willingly implemented and supported solutions they formulated. Practice saying "Bring Me Your Solutions and Not Your Problems" (BMYSANYP). I picked this suggestion up from a conference I attended several years ago. I put the letters "BMYSANYP" on my office door.

Keep a Reminder/Idea Box

To keep up with ideas or things that come to your mind, keep a 3" × 5" index file on your desk. Jot down ideas and things you want to remember. You would be surprised at the number of ideas that will come to your mind during the course of a day. I would even use my file to remind myself of changes I needed to make in our parent/student and staff handbooks. Use an alphabetical or monthly file to organize your ideas and reminders.

Grow Personally and Professionally

Read! Read! Read! Take time to read literature that will help you grow as a person and as an educator. Invest in several books on tape so you can even grow as you drive to and from work. I cannot think of a better way to unwind and leave the cares of the world and your job behind!

Connect Spiritually

Regardless of your religious affiliations or beliefs, spend quality time meditating, praying, and communicating with your inner spirit. Recognize that God has a plan for each of us on this earth. He has endowed each of us with special gifts and talents. We must use the gifts to help someone and improve mankind in general.

Your role as a school administrator is very powerful and influential. Whatever you say or do may impact or affect a child for the rest of his or her life. Connecting spiritually keeps you humble and keeps your heart and mind in the right place at all times. Always strive to do your best and put your best foot forward each day.

Never lose sleep at night worrying about how you treated someone or what you said to a staff member, student, or parent. Start each day on your knees, and you will be able to stand tall and face whatever comes your way.

For me, my belief in Almighty God has been a source of strength, comfort, and consolation during turbulent times throughout my personal and professional life. In my estimation, connecting spiritually is the most important survival tool needed. It lays the foundation for everything we do throughout the rest of our lives.

Concluding Remarks from the Author

This two-year writing project has been a labor of love and sheer adventure for me. Sometimes I even found myself laughing out loud as I recalled some of my experiences. I hope that many of my suggested practices and worksheets will be a good resource for new and continuing school administrators. I tried to add a personal, realistic down-to-earth touch to the handbook. I would love to receive feedback from other first-year or continuing school administrators and educational leadership instructors. If you would like to share your experiences, ideas, or worksheets with me, please forward them to the address below.

Dr. Sheila E. Sapp
202 Tiffany Circle
St. Marys, Georgia 31558
Fax: 912-882-0803
E-mail: sesapp@gate.net

Appendix 1—Sample Forms

CROOKED RIVER ELEMENTARY SCHOOL
DISCIPLINARY REFERRAL FORM

School Year _____

STUDENT _____   GRADE _____

PARENT(S) TELEPHONE # (HOME)_____   WORK _____

DATE/TIME _____

TEACHER _____

REASON(S) FOR REFERRAL: (BE BRIEF AND SPECIFIC)

_____

_____

_____

_____

Previous Efforts to Correct Problem (write date of effort in blanks):

Checked student record _____

Isolated student _____

Referred for counseling _____

Developed behavior modification contract with student/parent (copy attached)

_____

Held conference with parent _____

Detained student after school _____

Consulted assistant principal _____

Sent previous report home _____

Held a student support team meeting _____

Held conference with student _____

Other: (Specify) _____

_____

Administrator's action taken and/or recommendation(s):

_____

_____

Rationale for action taken and/or recommendation(s):

_____

_____

Signature of principal _____

Date _____

Signature of assistant principal _____

Date _____

REQUEST TO LEAVE EARLY

NAME _____   DATE _____

TIME & DATE OF LEAVE   _____

REASON FOR REQUEST   _____

_____

_____

_____

_____
TEACHER'S SIGNATURE

APPROVED _____

NOT APPROVED _____

_____
ADMINISTRATOR'S SIGNATURE

For Office Use Only
IF NEEDED, SUBSTITUTE SECURED _____

Appendix 1—Sample Forms

MID-SIX-WEEK PROGRESS REPORT

CIRCLE:
REPORT NUMBER: 1   2   3   4   5   6   Date _____

Dear _____,

At the present time your child _____ _____ is doing less than satisfactory work in the following area(s):

Check area(s) below:

_____Reading   _____Science   _____Art

_____Math   _____Spelling   _____Music

_____English   _____Physical Ed.   _____Handwriting

_____Social Studies   _____Health   _____Other

Call the school and set up an appointment to see me to discuss the area(s) checked above. The office phone number is: _____

_____
Teacher's Signature

_____
Parent's Signature

_____
Student's Signature

CONFERENCE REPORT

Date: _____

Teacher: _____   Parent: _____

Team: _____   PTA: _____

Staff: _____   Other: _____

Date: _____

Time: _____

Length of Conference: _____

Subject of Conference:

_____

_____

Objective of Conference: (Purpose)

_____

_____

_____

_____

Result of Conference:

_____

_____

_____

_____

Parent's Signature: _____

Teacher's Signature: _____

Classroom Maintenance
Requests or Furniture Needs

Teacher _____   Grade _____

Maintenance Need/Request:

_____

_____

_____

_____

Furniture Need/Request:

_____

_____

_____

_____

Approved   Yes _____   No _____

Comments:

_____

_____

_____

_____

ACTIVITY RESOURCE PERSON
REQUEST FORM

TYPE _____

VISITOR'S (RESOURCE PERSON'S) NAME _____

OCCUPATION _____

INSTRUCTIONAL OBJECTIVES BEING ADDRESSED:

_____

TIME _____   DATE _____

LOCATION(S) _____

_____
TEACHER'S SIGNATURE

_____
ADMINISTRATOR'S SIGNATURE

APPROVED _____

DENIED   _____

TEAM MEETING MINUTES

GRADE-LEVEL TEAM _____

DATE _____   TIME _____ to _____   LOCATION _____

AGENDA   TEAM MEMBERS ATTENDING

A. _____   1. _____

_____   2. _____

B. _____   3. _____

_____   4. _____

C. _____   5. _____

_____   OTHERS PRESENT

D. _____   1. _____

_____   2. _____

E. _____   3. _____

_____   4. _____

NOTES:

A. _____

_____

B. _____

_____

C. _____

_____

D. _____

_____

E. _____

_____

_____
TEAM LEADER

Dear Parent/Visitor:

The _____ administration, faculty, and staff sustain the belief that through a strong curriculum, a positive atmosphere, a high standard of teaching, and community support, the students taught will fully achieve mastery. We welcome your interest in our school. Our goal is to provide the best learning environment possible for our students. In order to ensure a planned and meaningful classroom visit, we have formulated the following guidelines:

1. Contact the school to schedule an observation with the teacher.

2. Instruction will proceed according to teacher direction with no interruptions or distractions from the observer.

3. If you would like to schedule a conference after the observation, please contact the school principal.

We hope to increase the understanding of the learning process and our curriculum by implementing the above guidelines. A better understanding of our curriculum and instructional process will build a stronger link with the school, home, and community.

I have read and agree to follow the guidelines above:

Signature: _____

Date: _____

Appendix 2—
Sample "We Believe" Statements

Students

- We believe every child has the ability to learn.
- We believe each child has a basic goodness.
- We believe each child is unique in his or her own way.
- We believe each child's individual thoughts and feelings are important.
- We believe each child brings his/her own life experiences to the classroom.

Community

- We believe that it is our professional obligation to present ourselves and our school to the community in the best light.

- We believe that the community and school should work together as a team to provide a more sound education for all students.

- The community has many assets by which a school can enhance each child's education, such as our state parks, our historical district, our National Park Service, and Cumberland Island. We will use the community services in a more efficient manner by helping our faculty and staff become aware of these unique services.

Parents

- We believe that parents are a major asset to the child's education.
- We believe that parents should keep an open mind in dealing with their child's education.
- We believe that parents should keep a positive attitude about school and instill that attitude in their children.
- We believe that parents and teachers should work cooperatively for the best interests of their child.
- We believe that parents should devote quality time daily to attend to any needs of their child.

Learning

- We believe that learning should be fun.
- We believe that children learn by doing, learn from each other, and learn through their senses.
- We believe that all children learn in different ways and at different stages.
- We believe that all aspects of his/her environment affect a child's learning ability.
- We believe that learning is a continuous process.
- We believe that attitudes affect learning.

Suggested Readings

Acaro, Janice. 1995. *Creating Quality in the Classroom.* Delray Beach, Fla.: St. Lucie Press.

Ashbaugh, Carl R., and Katherine L. Kasten. 1995. *Educational Leadership: Case Studies for Reflective Practice.* White Plains, N.Y.: Longman Publishers.

Calabrese, Raymond L. 1996. *Hands-On Leadership Tools for Principals* (Leadership & Management Series). Princeton, N.J.: Eye on Education.

Click, Phyllis M. 1995. *Administration of Schools for Young Children.* Albany, N.Y.: Delmar Publishers.

Daresh, John D., and Marsha A. Playko. 1997. *Beginning the Principalship: A Practical Guide for New School Leaders.* Thousand Oaks, Calif.: Corwin Press.

Hughes, Larry W., and Gerald C. Ubben. 1994. *The Elementary Principal's Handbook: A Guide to Effective Action.* Boston: Allyn and Bacon.

Lunenburg, Fred C., and Frederick Lunenburg. 1995. *The Principalship: Concepts and Applications.* Englewood Cliffs, N.J.: Prentice-Hall.

Norton, Marcia N., and Gene St. Paul. 1985. *Principals Resource Book.* Englewood Cliffs, N.J.: Prentice-Hall.

Thorpe, Ronald. 1995. *The First Year as Principal: Real World Stories from America's Principals.* Portsmouth, N.H.: Heinemann Publishers.

Wendel, Fredrick C. *Outstanding School Administrators: Their Keys to Success.* West Port, Conn.: Praeger.

About the Author

Sheila E. Sapp, a former elementary school teacher, reading specialist, instructional supervisor, assistant principal, and principal, resides in St. Marys, Georgia, with her husband, Everette. Sapp is the director of elementary curriculum for Camden County School System in Kingsland, Georgia. She is a member of the Georgia Council of Compensatory Education Leaders, Georgia Association of Educators, Georgia Association of Educational Leaders, Association of Supervision and Curriculum Development, Georgia International Reading Association, and the National Association for the Education of Young Children.